Flowers in the Field

Flowers
in the Field

How to find, identify and enjoy wild flowers

Faith Anstey

with photographs by Polly Pullar

Whittet Books

Whittet Books Ltd
BSP House, Station Road
Linton, Cambs CB21 4NW
email: mail@whittetbooks.com

First published 2010
Text © 2010 Faith Anstey
Photographs © Individual photographers indicated in the credits

A catalogue record for this book is available from the British Library.

ISBN 978 1 873580 80 6

Designed by Lodge Graphics

Printed and bound in China by WKT

CONTENTS

INTRODUCTION

Imagine you're taking a country walk with friends or family (choose your own spot from the south coast to the Scottish hills). Someone points out an attractive wild flower and says, 'You're interested in nature, aren't you? What's this flower called, do you know?'

'Well, not exactly, but I've got a book here . . . let's see . . . the flowers are yellow and they've got, er, five petals . . . I'll soon find it.'

As you search through the pictures in the fieldguide, it seems as though every other flower in Britain must be yellow with five petals. You're sure it's not a buttercup or a primrose. But then there are about a dozen of these cinquefoils, four or five saxifrages, at least six kinds of loosestrife and several others, all with five yellow petals. By the time you've found the page showing St John's worts and decided your specimen has got to be one of those, everyone else has moved away, while you're still wondering which of the many St John's worts it could be.

Two different, but very similar-looking, species of **St John's wort.**

Not wanting to be left behind, but now fired with curiosity, you hastily pluck one of the flowers and pop it in your pocket: you can have a closer look in the fieldguide when you get home. But when you do, doubts begin to creep in. St John's worts have pairs of leaves opposite each other - but you don't know, because in your haste, you only picked the flower itself. And even if you have found the right group, how can you answer the questions the book poses: Is the plant hairy? (Hard to say when it's all squashed.) Is it growing in acid soil? (How should I know?) Has it got a square stem? (I give up.)

If that scenario touches any chords, then this book is for you. You want to know more about wild flowers, and you want to be able to give names to the ones you find. 'What's in a name?' you may ask. But being able to 'name that plant' is just the beginning.

Once you have a name for a particular plant, you can:

- tell someone else what it is
- recognise it the next time you see it
- picture it when you come across a reference to it
- accurately label photographs, sketches and so on
- start keeping records of what you have found.

As you get more plant names under your belt, you will probably find other questions springing to mind, such as:

Why does this plant grow here (in a field, for example) and not there (in a wood)?

Will I find this plant as easily in Cumbria as in Cornwall, say?

How come buttercups are so common, when orchids are not? And perhaps

Why is there so much fuss about Japanese knotweed?

Buttercups are common, but **orchids** are not.

Japanese knotweed
looms over another invasive alien,
Himalayan balsam.

One aim of this book is to encourage you to ask questions like these. It won't provide you with all the answers, but it will offer a solid background of understanding, so that you can work out many of the answers for yourself.

As you learn more, you will find you can:

- understand better how plants relate to their habitats and to each other
- go on field trips with increased confidence
- pursue a specialist interest involving plants
- look out for plants in a deeper sense: in other words, feel a responsibility for their survival.

No previous in-depth knowledge of plants is assumed. The first time a technical term or specialised meaning is introduced, it will be printed in **bold**, and a definition or explanation will follow. Nor do you need to have reached any particular level in the study of plants. I doubt you'd be reading this book if you couldn't actually tell a foxglove from a buttercup, so we'll take it from there. But did you know, for example, that while we only have a single species of foxglove in this country, we have half-a-dozen common kinds (species) of buttercup - several of which you might easily come across on a country walk?

*In this country, we have only a single species of native **foxglove**.*

As well as having only one native foxglove in the British Isles; we also have only a single native bluebell and only one true wild strawberry. In most cases. though, one English name covers a number of species: besides six common species of buttercup, there are a similar number of common thistles and of common forget-me-nots. The total number of plant species in the British Isles is around two and a half thousand, and worldwide there may be up to half a million, many as yet undiscovered. An alarming quarter of all species is at risk of extinction, so we need to learn as much as possible about plants to give them a better chance of survival.

The large numbers involved may seem intimidating at first, but once reduced to smaller groups in a systematic way - this book shows you how - the task of identifying any given plant becomes much more manageable.

There is only one common plant with the English name **'primrose'**, although cowslips and oxlips are closely related to it. But see page 12 for the very rare Scottish primrose.

Maybe you don't expect to get any further than saying 'It's a forget-me-not' or 'It's an orchid'. On the other hand, perhaps you're immensely keen to know which forget-me-not or orchid you have found. In either case, this book sets out to put you on the right track.

There are all sorts of reasons why people take an interest in wild flowers. Perhaps you just like to walk in the countryside and want to add to your pleasure by being able to identify the flowers you encounter. Maybe you are keen on conservation of the environment and its inhabitants. On the other hand, perhaps your hobbies involve painting or photographing the natural world. Your interest and enjoyment will be increased tenfold if you know something of the lifestyle and relationships of the flowers you see. And if by any chance what you want to do is eat plant products or make medicinal concoctions from them, then you absolutely must get the knowledge before you poison yourself.

In this book I hope to encourage all these endeavours by explaining the basic facts about wild flowers - what they are, where they grow and how they live. Once you start plant-finding or **botanising**, you have embarked on an interest that may well last you all your life. Botanising is simply the insider's name for what people do when they study wild plants 'in the field' (or in the wood, by the river, anywhere out of doors). You don't need to be an expert - just an enthusiast.

Participants in a **local botanical outing** enjoying an important part of the day - the picnic lunch.

WHAT IS A WILD FLOWER?

This book deals mainly with examples and generalisations from plants that can be found growing wild in the British Isles and commonly called 'wild flowers'. But what exactly counts as a 'wild flower'? Daisies, dandelions and buttercups are easily recognised as being wild flowers (even if they're growing on your lawn) but let's pause here for a moment and consider what we really mean by 'wild flowers'. First of all, what is 'wild'?

WILDNESS

What counts as a wild plant? Obviously, something you have deliberately planted and nurtured in your garden is not a wild plant. At the other extreme, a plant that has been growing undisturbed on a Pennine peak since time immemorial is surely a wild plant. But what of everything in between? This is actually rather a controversial question in botanical circles. Some botanists are less interested in plants that are not true primordial natives, while others are fascinated by the changes in our flora, possibly accelerated by global warming and other trends. Where to draw the line can be more a matter of opinion, so to help you make your own decision, consider the following points.

WILD OR NOT?	
CATEGORY	EXAMPLE
native all over the British isles	daisy, primrose, dog rose
native to some places, introduced in others	Welsh poppy, tutsan, meadow cranesbill
introduced before 1500 CE	spearmint, cornflower, hemlock
introduced after 1500, now established	ivy-leaved toadflax, snowdrop, fox-and-cubs
casual i.e. not reproducing successfully in the wild	garden throw-outs needing human attention

Fox-and-cubs may be the bane of many gardeners, owing to its determinedly spreading habit. However, as one of our few truly orange flowers - native or alien - it is hard not to have a sneaking fondness for it.

Snowdrops can be seen in woods and hedgerows throughout most of the country, but are they really as wild as they seem?

Introduced plants are often called **aliens** (nothing to do with ET). 'Introduced' can mean that the plant

- was deliberately planted in the wild
- has escaped from gardens
- was brought from abroad as a food or medicinal plant
- has sprouted from domestic birdseed
- entered by accident along with textile or grain imports etc.
- even was transported on botanists' boots!

In a broader sense, all British plants are 'introductions'. During the last Ice Age - up to about 10,000 years ago - there were few if any plants here, perhaps one or two left stranded at the tops of mountain peaks clear of ice. All colonisation by plants has taken place since that time, and the process is still continuing. Many older introductions such as field forget-me-nots have a native air to them by now: perhaps in 500 years time, we will feel the same about Japanese knotweed. (Or perhaps not.)

The problem is that alien plants may begin to spread at the expense of natives. Some are very vigorous and may crowd out the plants that used to be found at that spot, often creating a monoculture along roadsides and riverbanks.

Himalayan balsam *may colonise long stretches of riverbank and damp woodland, crowding out late-flowering natives.*

The 'big three' offenders in this respect are giant hogweed, Japanese knotweed and Himalayan (Indian) balsam. Many people would also include rhododendron and invasive water plants such as New Zealand pigmyweed originating from garden ponds. We need to ask ourselves exactly what harm aliens are doing, what plants they are replacing and how they can be controlled if necessary.

UNIQUE TO BRITAIN
At the opposite end of the scale to aliens are the British endemics. These are the native plants that grow nowhere else in the world, so their loss in these islands would be a global tragedy. There are about a dozen British endemics, some examples being the Scottish primrose, wild cotoneaster (Wales) and the Lundy cabbage. The Lundy cabbage, which grows only on the island of Lundy in the Bristol Channel, even has its very own endemic insect which can live on no other plant. Hard work has been carried out to reduce the menace of introduced rhododendron on the island. However, the Lundy cabbage (and its minibugs) is now threatened by bracken and rabbits.

Although 'wild' is clearly a rather controversial term, you might think that 'flower' is quite straightforward.
But read on...

Lundy cabbage is, one must admit, not a very exciting-looking plant, but the **endemic Scottish primrose** is a stunning sight.

Perennial cornflower often escapes from gardens, but rarely ventures very far. The annual cornflower (somewhat smaller) has been known as an arable weed in Britain since the Iron Age but is now mostly a product of wildflower seed mixes.

FLOWERING PLANTS

Plants can be divided into two basic kinds: flowering and non-flowering. However, the group of flowering plants includes many more plants than those we usually call 'flowers'. Grasses and sedges, vegetables and crops, most trees and shrubs are flowering plants. Think of the blossom on a cherry tree, or of fields glowing with the fluorescent yellow of a rape crop. Visualise a vegetable patch where the rhubarb has sprouted a tall spike of creamy flowers, or a conservatory full of tomato plants in flower, promising a good crop of fruit later on. Perhaps, in early summer, you've noticed a whole meadow or verge turn overnight to a shimmering haze of pink or mauve as grasses suddenly come into flower.

Although these are all flowering plants, we tend to think of them in terms of other characteristics first. Trees may be valued for their timber, vegetables are important for our food, crops may be grown for their fibres, grass as feed for livestock and so on. But from a botanist's point of view, whatever their size, shape or uses, if they bear flowers then they are flowering plants.

Conversely, flowering plants always have flowers. You may hear someone confidently assert 'Oh, that one [it's often a tree] doesn't have flowers'. But that will only be true if the tree is a conifer; other trees are flowering plants as well. The fact is that the flowers may be small and insignificant, like those of

*Though mainly encountered as a hedge plant, a fully grown **hawthorn** or **may tree** is a beautiful sight - and now it's out you can change a clout.*

*This grass is called **Yorkshire fog**. 'Fog' because when it comes into flower, as here, it looks as though a low-lying pinkish mist has settled on the field. Why 'Yorkshire'? No-one seems to know, as it is abundant everywhere, not just in Yorkshire.*

grasses and many trees. Or the flowers may be rare; some cacti-like plants, for example, only flower once in a lifetime. Some plants like nettles have green flowers which may be difficult to distinguish from the leaves or other green parts. All flowering plants do have flowers, even if you can't find them at that moment.

So we see that flowering plants *have* flowers, rather than *are* flowers. In ordinary speech we use the word 'flower' to mean both the complete plant and the showy colourful bit with petals. However, to avoid confusion we will here be confining 'flower' to the second meaning. This book is about **wild flowering plants**. When we talk about 'flowers' it will usually be in contrast to other parts of the plant, such as root, leaves or stem.

Cherry blossom *demonstrates vividly that deciduous trees are flowering plants too.*

TREES, SHRUBS AND HERBS

*Although these are sometimes called the 'flowers' of the **larch**, they are not true flowers, but immature cones.*

As we have seen, most trees are flowering plants; that is to say, they bear flowers at some time or other. The exceptions are those usually called **conifers** (cone-bearers), such as pines, firs and cypresses. Conifers do not have proper flowers (although they do have pollen). These trees are sometimes known colloquially as 'evergreens', but this is misleading, since some flowering plants are also green throughout the year.

So what exactly makes a tree a tree? Surprisingly, it's quite difficult to give a precise botanical definition of a tree, although some botanists do try to lay down the law about it. In general, a **tree** is a plant with a single tall woody trunk. A **shrub** is a plant with several

***Trees** - these are birches - normally have a single trunk and live for many years. Apart from the conifers, trees are **flowering plants**.*

woody stems. However, when trees are growing in demanding conditions, such as on mountains, they may make take a much more shrub-like form: mountain willows, birches and junipers, for example, creep along the ground instead of growing upright. Trees are generally longer-lived than other plants, and rather than completing a cycle each year, they may take many years to begin producing flowers and fruit.

Herbs, in contrast, are not just the plants you flavour your casserole with. Herbs are all the flowering plants which do *not* have a woody stem, and they *do* have a seasonal cycle. They either retreat at the end of the flowering season to pass the winter close to or under the ground, or they die completely and rely on their seeds to begin a new cycle in the following year. (More about life cycles on page 49.) Your daisies, dandelions and buttercups are all examples of herbs.

However, grasses and sedges are also herbs, since they are flowering plants without woody stems and with an annual cycle. People who are new to botany usually find grasses much more difficult to identify than other flowering plants, chiefly because their flowers are very small and rudimentary, with none of the showy and colourful petals that are so helpful in identifying other plants. Herbs other than grasses and sedges are technically called **forbs**, and it is the forbs which we will mainly be studying in this book. When people talk about 'wild flowers' it is usually the forbs they mean, though this is not a word in everyday use.

It is probably a good plan to get to grips with the more vivid colours and distinctive forms of the forbs to begin with. Once you have absorbed the basics and your appetite is whetted, you can continue with shrubs and trees, or perhaps tackle the trickier sedges, rushes and grasses.

Tricky to identify, perhaps, but so attractive: **grasses, sedges and rushes**.

NON-FLOWERING PLANTS

As we shall see in the next chapter, flowers are the mechanism by which flowering plants reproduce. Non-flowering plants (which evolved earlier) have different lifestyles, and approach the business of reproduction by other means. Botanists study non-flowering plants as well as flowering ones, of course, but most field botanists - those who botanise out of doors, rather than doing research in a laboratory - tend to concentrate mainly on flowering plants. (If you want to know more about, say, ferns or mosses, there are books which are devoted to these plants.) The table below gives examples of the two contrasting groups.

Horsetails *are **non-flowering plants**. Some horsetails have long branches, making them look rather like miniature trees. Others have no branches at all up the sectioned stems.*

FLOWERING PLANTS	NON-FLOWERING PLANTS
broad-leaved trees	conifers
shrubs	ginkgos & cycads
forbs ('flowers')	ferns
grasses	horsetails
sedges & rushes	mosses

N.B. Fungi, algae (seaweeds etc.) and lichens are no longer classified as plants at all.

Cottongrass is not a grass at all but a sedge. The cottony heads are the fruits, the equivalent of dandelion clocks. This picture also shows species of rushes and mosses. Grasses, sedges and rushes are all flowering plants, but mosses are non-flowering.

THE PLANT THAT WASN'T

Confusion about what is a plant at all may even reach rock bottom, so to speak. You may have seen advertisements for a so-called houseplant, the Neptune plant, which is described as a 'botanical wonder of nature' found on the ocean bed. It is green, but never needs watering, emits fragrant secretions which drive away flies and 'is unable to be classified in any botanical category.' Wondering how this could possibly be so, I put the question to readers of a botanical journal and this was the answer: because it's not a plant at all - it's an animal! It is actually a colony of the dead bodies of Hydrozoa - something like a soft coral reef. One reader commented that it was rather like saying that 'rock buns are unable to be classified by geologists'.

Is it a bird? Is it a plane? No, and it's not a plant either. The so-called **Neptune plant** is the remains of minute undersea animals, the soft green equivalent of a coral reef.

HOW FLOWERS WORK

Flowering plants have flowers. The most straightforward way to identify a plant is by its flower. But what exactly is a flower? It's usually colourful - but not necessarily, as we have seen. It's usually obvious - but again, not always. It's often at the top of the plant - but equally often it is not. It's the part that normally appears in spring and withers away later in the year - you're getting warmer. A **flower** is the reproductive apparatus of a flowering plant. Now you're talking!

All living things need to reproduce by some method or other, and higher forms do so sexually. That is, they make use of the differences between male and female to create the next generation. (Although all flowering plants can reproduce sexually, some don't always bother, but use asexual methods such as spreading underground to pop up nearby.)

STRUCTURE OF A FLOWER

When getting to grips with botany, it is vital to take a practical attitude. Botanising just cannot be done indoors with only a book for company. So at this point I highly recommend you to do something, namely, to collect a specimen that you can refer to while you are reading, so that you really understand what is going on. For the moment, it doesn't matter whether your flower is wild or not, as we're just looking at the structure, so a garden flower or 'weed' will do fine.

The best kind of specimen would be one with a simple shape such as a violet, primrose or forget-me-not. Avoid the daisy/dandelion type for the moment as they are not typical. But always choose from something there is plenty of, and don't pick any more than you need. For a fuller explanation of how to pick flowers from the wild without damaging the species or its habitat, see page 131. The example chosen here is herb robert: it grows almost everywhere near habitation for a large part of the year, so you may well be able to find a specimen to compare with the pictures. If not, choose something similar that's close to hand.

Herb robert *is very common around buildings and as a garden weed, but also found in woods and hedgerows, and on shingle and scree. Its ubiquity is due to it being equally happy in sunshine or shade, on dry ground or damp, earthy or stony.*

It would also be a great help to provide yourself with the only piece of special equipment a botanist really needs, namely, a **lens**. A x10 hand lens (one that magnifies by ten) is ideal. However, the sort used for map-reading or embroidery is better than nothing. Botanical booksellers and opticians generally sell lenses. With a lens, you can study all the tiny details that help to identify plants. You may also find yourself marvelling at the amazing complexity and intricacy of nature.

WHAT IS A WEED?

A weed is often defined as 'a plant growing in the wrong place', although you may prefer Emerson's version: 'a plant whose virtues have not yet been discovered'. However, a number of plants which any gardener would classify as weeds do indeed have virtues. You could feast on dandelion wine, nettle soup or chickweed salad, for example. Ground elder, one of the most universally loathed of garden weeds, was introduced by the Romans as a vegetable. Comfrey, which appears uninvited in many gardens, has been demonstrated to have healing properties - reflected in its alternative name of 'knitbone' - to the extent that some some livestock owners deliberately encourage it in their fields, as horses and cattle will eat it readily. Unfortunately they can be just as keen on ragwort, which is highly poisonous to them. (The word 'weed' comes from the same Old English root as 'wort', simply meaning a herb; ragwort is sometimes also known as ragweed.) And don't forget that the scarlet poppies which symbolise the tragedy of war sprang up in the trenches and shell-holes of Flanders, when the former arable land of which they had been 'weeds' became, to put it mildly, disturbed ground.

Redshank and *hemp nettle* are common weeds of arable land. They can often be found in gateways or on headlands where the weed spray has not reached.

Beware: at this stage, there are exceptions to almost all the generalisations one can make about plants! If your specimen is a little different from the description below, check again to make sure you're studying the right bit, then just make a mental note, or compare it with another kind of flower.

We're going to look at our specimen by starting in the middle, so to examine it properly you are probably going to have to remove a few petals so that you can observe the centre clearly. (If you're like me, you somehow hate doing this, but it is in the interests of science).

Right in the very centre of the herb robert flower is a part that looks like this:

Your specimen will have something corresponding to this, though it could be a different shape or colour. This is the female organ of the flower, consisting of the **stigma** (which in this case is red), held aloft by the **style**, which leads down to the **ovary**. These three parts together are called the **carpel** (**pistil** if more than one set). The purpose of the stigma is to collect pollen (the flower's version of sperm) so it often has a fuzzy or furry surface that the pollen will easily stick to. The pollen is transferred down the style to the ovary, where 'eggs' (ovules) await insemination. The ovary will eventually give rise to the fruit.

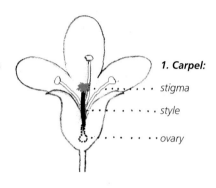

1. Carpel:

stigma

style

ovary

Moving outwards from the centre, the next structures are the male parts: the **stamens**. These have **anthers** at the top, which are brownish in the case of herb robert. The anthers are reservoirs of pollen and are poised at the top of the **filaments** (fine structures like the filament in a light bulb) so that the pollen can easily get carried away to rendezvous with a stigma. The pollen of a particular flower may be transferred to that flower's own stigma, but it is more usual for it to be taken (by insects or the wind) to another flower of the same species.

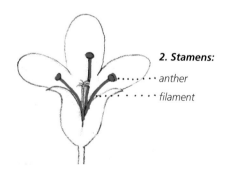

2. Stamens:

anther

filament

Why is it important to know which are the female parts and which are the male? When you have a plant you want to identify, these parts can sometimes hold vital clues. For example, one group of 5-petalled flowers can often be separated from another similar group according to whether they have just 5 or 10 stamens (male, outer ring) or whether the stamens are too many to count. Loosestrifes have only 5 stamens, but St John's worts have an uncountable number. Buttercups also have numerous stamens, but they usually have a bunch of many carpels (female, right in the middle) whereas St John's worts appear to have just a single one.

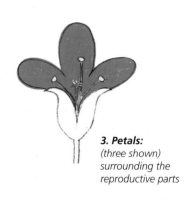

3. Petals:
(three shown)
surrounding the
reproductive parts

The stigma and stamens are what constitute the **flower**, in the strict sense. In most forbs, however, the stigma and stamens are surrounded by the **petals**. The reason petals are showy and colourful is to attract the insects which are going to transfer the pollen from one flower to another.

They sometimes do this in the process of drinking nectar from deep inside the flower (which is why plants have nectar in the first place). Grasses, and many tree flowers, are pollinated by the wind, so they don't need showy petals. On some petals, you will see 'honey guides' - fine lines or patterns which help direct the insect to the centre of the flower. Petals come in a myriad of colours, shapes, sizes and disguises and there are many different ways for flowers to arrange their petals, as we shall see shortly.

Next in line as we move outwards are the **sepals**. These protect the flower in the bud and may help to support it when it is open. They are usually green, but occasionally they are the same colour as the petals. However, they are always present in the kind of flowers we are discussing, so if you can't see any green sepals outside the petals, check whether they might be masquerading as petals. What appear to be the petals of a poppy, for example, are actually all coloured sepals. In other flowers, the petals and sepals look identical, in which case they may be known as **tepals**.

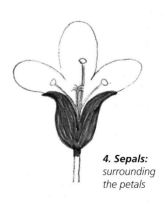

4. Sepals:
surrounding
the petals

By the way, if you are feeling bogged down in so many terms that begin with S---, rest assured that most botany students feel the same.

A mnemonic (memory aid) would be useful, but as far as I know, no-one has ever come up with a good one, except perhaps for the pun that 'stamens stay men'. The best way to learn new words is to keep using them, of course, so whenever you study a flower you could be saying to yourself, 'That's the stigma, those are the stamens' and so on.

*As this **scabious** flower begins to open, the **stamens** can be clearly seen, with their pollen-laden **anthers** at the tips.*

*This **marsh marigold**, a member of the Buttercup family, has numerous **stamens** surrounding a clump of **carpels** in the centre.*

A few more technical terms that you might encounter in your fieldguide are:

corolla = set of petals

calyx = set of sepals

perianth = petals & sepals together

Monkeyflowers
(right) have a short
calyx tube *of sepals*
which is almost
as yellow as the
corolla *of petals.*
Red campions
(below) have a long
slender ***calyx tube***
of dark red sepals,
surrounding the
bright pink ***corolla**.*

Thus we have the basic structure of the flower itself. Where identification is concerned, it is important to study any plant you find, looking for the parts we have mentioned, so that you aren't fooled by leaves that look like petals, petals that look like leaves and so on (plants are up to all kinds of tricks like these!) There are many other characteristics which will help you identify your specimen, and we will come on to these in the next section. Before that, we will examine the basic types of flower.

THEMES AND VARIATIONS

When you start on the process of identifying a particular specimen, you need to be able to narrow the field progressively until you can confidently home in on the correct group, and eventually (hopefully) the exact species. At this point, it would be a good idea to collect one or two more specimens of different kinds of flowering plants - genuinely wild ones this time - to compare with the descriptions and illustrations that follow. A good selection could include a dandelion or daisy, a violet or speedwell, a clover or mint and a bluebell or iris. But if you are taking plants home to study, choose something that is very common: a good rule of thumb for conservation is to count twenty of exactly the same kind before you pick just one. (And, of course, pick it only - uprooting any plant, unless in your own garden, is against the law.)

It would also be a good idea at this stage to have a fieldguide to hand, so that you can make plenty of comparisons between different species to help you understand the various features. See the discussion on pages 96-7 for hints on choosing a fieldguide.

Flowers - as opposed to leaves, stems, roots etc. - show the most obvious individuality, so we begin here with the basic features of flowers.

Flower colour

The colour of a flower's petals is often the most striking thing about it and it may look like an easy option just to trawl through the fieldguide playing 'snap'. Two caveats here, though. In the first place, the limitations of the printing process mean that colours in books, whether paintings or photographs, may not always be quite true to nature. Secondly, it is quite common for flowers to appear in non-standard colours. Blue flowers, in particular, may be 'also in white' due to the absence of certain pigments. Bluebells, forget-me-nots and milkworts, for example, regularly come in mauve, pink or white versions, but could be exactly the same species as the blue variety. So take a note of the colour, of course, but don't rely on it exclusively in your ID (identification) task.

'Also in white'. In some places, **white foxgloves** outnumber the standard purple ones, but they are all the same species.

*This **birds-nest orchid** has no green colouring because it does not photosynthesise (see page 38). It gets its nourishment not from the sun, but via fungi in the soil.*

*The glorious colour of **autumn leaves** is due to green pigment fading, allowing the underlying red and yellow pigments to be displayed.*

COATS OF MANY COLOURS

In the summer countryside we are surrounded by green vegetation, a background in which coloured flowers stand out. We see flowers in red, yellow, blue and so on because of our eye/brain reaction to whichever part of the sunlight spectrum is reflected from their surfaces. The light which is not reflected is absorbed, and this is the part of the spectrum used by the plant for producing energy.

So the fact that we see plants in glorious technicolour is a by-product of the plants' own need to capture energy from sunlight. To us this makes flowers beautiful - and identifiable. To insects (and a few other creatures) it makes them attractive as signifying 'here is pollen, here is nectar'. Plants that are pollinated by wind rather than insects - notably grasses - do not waste resources on brightly-coloured petals to set off their flowers.

Totally parasitic plants, such as broomrapes, derive all their nourishment from the hosts on which they live, so they don't need much in the way of pigments. In particular, their vegetative parts - leaves, sepals, stems etc. - are not green. Other plants have green vegetative parts because they contain the pigment chlorophyll, which is the main instrument for converting sunlight to energy. In the autumn, chlorophyll production wanes and the colours of other pigments show up instead. The other notable pigments are carotenoids (yellow/orange/red) and anthocyanins (red/purple/blue). Besides supplying the reds and yellows of autumn leaves, these pigments also give flowers their colours.

Design of flower

The arrangement of petals in a flower can vary enormously, but tends to run in families, so again you can narrow your search by deciding what category the overall design of the flower falls into. We shall simplify matters here by looking at five basic designs which between them cover most of the possibilities. The five are:

Composite   **All-round symmetry**   **Mirror symmetry**   **Bell-shaped**   **Lipped**

Composites are members of the Aster family, and typical representatives are daisies, thistles and dandelions. A **composite** flowerhead appears to be a single flower, but in fact it is made up of a large number of tiny flowers arranged as a core with surrounding circles. Look very closely - preferably through your lens - at one of these and you will find that each of the 'petals' (properly known as florets) has its own stamen and/or stigma, so each one is a separate flower in its own right. A composite flower is a very special design, unlike any other.

*A **composite** flower is made up of many tiny flowers, often of two different types, as in the rays (white) and discs (yellow) of this oxeye daisy. Each ray and disc has its own stamen and/or style.*

However, as it has much the appearance of a single flower, once you grasp how it is constructed it can be treated like other flowers in the descriptions that follow.

***All-round symmetry**, like a plate or saucer shape, is shown by these bloody (epithet, not expletive) cranesbills.*

Composites are special cases of the next design we look at, namely, **all-round symmetry**. These are flowers shaped like a plate or saucer (if more like a cup, see 'bell-shaped'). They look the same whether viewed from top, bottom, left or right. Many species such as roses, primroses, buttercups and geraniums (including the herb robert we studied earlier) have all-round symmetrical flowers. However, the individual petals can be pointed or rounded, overlapping or spaced out, notched, split or wavy-edged and so on. So these features can be used to narrow down your search among all-round symmetrical flowers.

Mirror symmetry is one step away from all-round symmetry. Here you only get two identical halves if you divide the flower from top to bottom. If you divide from side to side, you will find that the lower part of the flower is not quite - or not at all - the same as the upper part: the lower part may be a different shape, size or colour. Examples of mirror symmetry are violets, speedwells and monkeyflowers.

Pansies and violets are examples of mirror symmetry flowers. Divided vertically, the two halves are mirror images of each other, but the top half is different from the bottom half.

*This **harebell** has five petals joined into a **bell**.*

A different kind of all-round symmetry, **bell-shaped** is fairly self-explanatory: the petals are (or look as though they are) joined into the shape of a bell, cup, flask or trumpet. Examples are bluebells, harebells, gentians and heathers.

Lipped flowers come in many varieties, somewhat in the shape of a mouth, which may be open or closed, or more like a face with a mouth, nose and ears. Like a face, they usually have mirror symmetry also.

The orchid on this page clearly shows the lipped shape. These flowers look rather like those of mints and deadnettles, but read on to explore the crucial difference between them.

*Orchid flowers are always some variation on the **lipped** design, the lip in this case being known as the labellum. But how to distinguish orchids from other lipped flowers? Orchids are **monocots**.*

HOW ODD!

Which flowers have the most unusual designs? The orchids immediately spring to mind, with flowers apparently mimicking bees, flies, frogs and so on. Incidentally, it is a bit of a misconception that each orchid is pollinated by the creature it resembles. True, bee orchids may be pollinated by bees, though they are usually self-pollinating. Butterfly orchids are pollinated by moths and fly orchids by wasps. But frog orchids are not pollinated by frogs - and ghost orchids certainly not by ghosts! Among the easier-to-find species, what about honeysuckle with its upper lip like a fingerless glove? Then there's columbine with a curly pigtail (a spur) behind each petal. Goldilocks buttercup is another one to look out for: it almost always has some petals either missing or strangely distorted, each flower being slightly different from its neighbour.

*Garden **honeysuckle** may be the same species as wild honeysuckle - as seen here - or a more exotic kind.*

*It is always a delight to discover **butterfly orchids**. Although their flowers have the rather ethereal quality associated with butterflies, they are actually pollinated by night-flying moths, attracted by the scent.*

Number of petals

Flowering plants divide into two main sections, and the number of petals is one of the chief ways of telling which section a particular plant falls into. The two sections are commonly called **monocots** and **dicots** (pronounced *die*-cots). The only British natives which are outside this classification are the water-lilies, which you are unlikely to mistake for anything else. The

*The **net-veined leaves** of a **dicot** - pennywort - seen intermingled with the **blade-like leaves** of monocot grasses.*

petals and sepals of monocots always number 3 or 6; any other number is a dicot. The majority of flowering plants are dicots, so if you can definitely label an unknown species as a monocot, at a stroke you have cut down your ID possibilities to about one-sixth of the total.

*A common **dicot** - the familiar daisy - and an uncommon **monocot** - northern marsh orchid - seen growing cheek by jowl.*

The following table includes some other characteristics that help to distinguish between monocots and dicots.

MONOCOTS short for monocotyledons - one seed leaf	DICOTS dicotyledons - two seed leaves
flowers: petals/sepals always in multiples of 3	4, 5 or more petals/sepals
leaves: straight 'blade' or simple oval	can be simple or compound shape
veins on leaf: lengthways veins only, often only one sometimes 3 or more	veins usually branching or forming fan pattern
EXAMPLES lily, bluebell, iris, orchid, water plants (grasses, sedges & rushes are also monocots)	virtually everything else: poppy, clover, thistle etc., etc.

Typified Monocot: 6 petals (a multiple of 3), blade leaves with parallel veins.

Typified Dicot: 5 petals (the most common number), leaves with branching veins.

Size of flower

Your fieldguide will tell you the size of flower to expect, but how to measure it? Flowers with all-round symmetry are measured across the diameter, but other types may be measured from front to back or top to bottom: check which one the book is talking about.

You need to think in millimetres. If inches come more naturally to you, bear in mind that 1 inch = roughly 25 mm, and 10 cm = roughly 4 inches. Fieldguides often have measurements marked along the edge of a cover, but it helps to know the length of your finger joints or you could carry a small ruler. 'Big' and 'small' are obviously relative terms, but generally speaking 10 mm is a small flower (chickweed, say), 20 mm is medium (the average daisy), 5 cm is large (dog rose) and 10 cm is very large (yellow iris). If the individual flowers are very tiny and clustered together, it will probably be more useful to look at how they are arranged on the flowerhead: see next section.

Flowerheads

We have looked at how the petals are arranged in the flower; now to examine the way the flowers are arranged on the stem: the flowerhead. The technical name for a flowerhead is an **inflorescence**. There are a number of themes in flowerheads, and then there are even more variations on those themes. If we concentrate here on just five major blueprints, the rest will gradually fall into place as you come across them.

*The **yellow iris** or flag has one of the largest flowers of British native species. They can be up to 100 mm (4 inches) across.*

These five are:

- single flowers
- several flowers (from one upwards) on one stem
- flowers collected into a spike shape
- flowers in a rounded head
- flowers whorled round the stem.

Need to know: the **stem** is the main support of the plant (like the trunk of a tree). The stalk or **pedicel** grows from the stem to support the individual flower (if the stalk is branched, it is the final branch which counts as the pedicel).

Single flowers. Some species specialise in having one and only one flower on the stem, from the ground up. The stem is unbranched. Think daisies. (It would be very difficult to make daisy-chains if they were not like this.)

Several. Another plan is for the plant to have stems which branch, giving the opportunity for several individual flowers on the stem, each with its own pedicel.

Single flower

Think buttercups. It is a bit technical to spell out how this kind of arrangement shades into the more organised sort of flowerhead, so do remember this is an oversimplification. However, the more carefully you have to look, the better you'll know the next time.

Several flowers

Spike shape. Many flowerheads come in the shape of a cone or spike. In these, the flowers - often very small - are all together, either at the top of the stem, or at the ends

Spike shape

of branches. Examples of spike shapes are found in orchids, agrimony and bluebell.

Agrimony *has a very obvious* **spike** *arrangement of its flowers.*

Rounded head. The technical term for the commonest type of rounded head is the **umbel**. This sounds rather technical, until you associate it with an umbrella. The umbrella's handle is the plant stem; the spokes are

Umbel

the flower stalks, which in a true umbel branch again into sub-spokes; the cover of the umbrella is the layer of individual flowers crowning the whole. Examples of umbellifers (umbel-bearers) are cow parsley and hogweed. There are also **clustered** rounded heads, similar to the umbel, but without the sub-spokes, examples being clovers and onion flowers.

Hogweed *flowers show the structure of a true umbellifer: the main 'spokes' can be clearly seen, but each tiny flower also has its own 'sub-spoke'.*

Whorl.   On deadnettles, mints and their relatives, for example, the flowers are arranged in leafy whorls up the stem with lengths of bare stem in between.

Whorled flowers

*At first sight, this may look like a spike arrangement, but on closer inspection you will see that the flowers of **purple loosestrife** shown here are arranged in separate **whorls** up the stem.*

The story so far

If, as I recommend, you have a plant or two beside you as you read, you should now be able to answer the following questions:

Is it a monocot or a dicot?

What colour are the flowers?

Has the flower got all-round symmetry?

If so, is it a composite?

If not a composite, how many petals in each flower?

If not flat and symmetrical, is it bell-shaped, mouth-shaped, or what?

What size are the flowers?

How are they arranged on the stem - the inflorescence?

Suppose that my answers to the questions above were:

It's a dicot

The flowers are salmon pink

It is all-round symmetrical but not a composite

It has five petals, arranged in a cup shape

The flower is medium size

There are several flowers to each stem.

If I stumble upon water avens (known in some places as Granny's nightcap) while searching through my fieldguide, I may feel that everything's coming up roses, as it were. So at this point in the search for a label for your own specimen, you could leaf through the fieldguide, looking for a possible match. But before you get carried away, it would be worthwhile to take the information in the next section into account.

Water avens *has five separate petals, arranged in a symmetrical cup shape.*

THE GREEN PARTS

It is tempting to rely on the flowers alone when trying to identify flowering plants, but this method often ends in stalemate when several species have flowers that seem exactly alike. In order to avoid mistakes - and indeed to make the process of identification both easier and more fun - we need to look at a number of other important clues. In the next chapter, 'Where to look', we consider the questions of habitat and distribution: knowledge of where a plant is likely to be found can make all the difference between a correct and an incorrect identification. After all, if you think you've found a Jersey lily, but you happen to be botanising in the Lake District, you may need to revise your judgment! Here, however, we are still concerned with the features we can see directly: the 'green parts' such as leaves, stem and so on, technically called the **vegetative features**.

The flowers of these two thistle-type plants are very similar, but an inspection of the green parts soon distinguishes them. **Marsh thistle** *(left) has exceedingly spiny leaves and stem, whereas* **knapweed** *(above) has no prickles at all, being merely roughly hairy.*

At this stage, it is better not to pick anything, but to study the plant as it grows in the wild. 'Take the book to the plant, not the plant to the book' is a motto often advocated. Not only does this make good conservation sense, it makes good botanising sense: seeing the whole plant in its natural setting gives one a much better idea of its overall appearance, how it compares with others and how it fits into the habitat.

Plant size

First a quick word about judging plant size. The kind of informal yardsticks you need for overall plant size are things like the width of your hand, height to the top of your boots or to your waist and so on. Books often use a comparison with well-known flowers. For example, 'tall' could be represented by a foxglove, 'medium' by a bluebell, 'short' by a cowslip and 'low' by a daisy.

However, a plant may be taller or shorter than the book suggests, due to competition from other plants, lack of nourishment, shady versus sunny situation and so on.

While we're on the subject of flowers that clearly haven't read the book, remember to beware of other kinds of poor specimen, such as those that have been chewed by animals. Certain species are more prone to variation than others: some orchids, for example, often have quite a large range in the colour, shape and markings of their petals. You may even come across 'sports' where nature seems to have gone mad and produced a plant weirdly different from its neighbours. It's a good plan not to rely on the characteristics of just one specimen, but have a look around and see if it is typical of the population.

Bearberry has shiny, leathery leaves to guard against the harsh environment of high moors and mountainsides on which it grows.

LEAVES - A BALANCING ACT
Leaves are the food factory of the plant. They already contain chlorophyll - the pigment responsible for their green colouring - plus water drawn up from the roots. Now they absorb carbon dioxide from the air and, using the energy of sunlight absorbed at the same time, these ingredients are converted to carbohydrates by the process called photosynthesis.

Why a balancing act? Leaves have this vital function to perform, but they are out in all weathers and need to maintain a stable environment for the chemical processes taking place inside. So, for example, leaves in a hot, dry environment need to conserve precious moisture: they may therefore have a shiny, heat-reflecting surface, or a boundary layer of hairs trapping humidity, or an internal water-storage system (succulence). On the other hand, when there is heavy rain, leaves need to shed water, so may have a design that allows the water to run off readily from a 'drip tip'. If the essential sunlight is in short supply, leaves may be as large as is feasible, and have a staggered arrangement on the plant so that they don't shade each other. If it is windy, leaves could be torn off easily, so they may be divided or cut, to reduce wind resistance. Some leaves are even self-cleaning - the so-called 'lotus effect', where water droplets pick up foreign particles such as mould spores and roll them clear off the leaf.

Leaves

Leaves come in an enormous variety of shapes, sizes and arrangements. A good fieldguide will usually have drawings labelling the different types. Here we concentrate on two factors:

- the composition of the leaves

- their relationship to the stem.

Composition. Simple leaves come one at a time: each has its own stalk direct to the stem. The leaves may be long and narrow (lanceolate), oval, round, heart-shaped, kidney-shaped and so on. The edges of the leaf (called the margins) may be wavy or toothed, or taken to extremes they can be lobed or deeply cut. **Compound** leaves, on the other hand, consist of a number of separate leaflets, arranged in a regular pattern. For example, they may be in pairs up the leaf stalk like the leaflets of an ash tree, or fanned out like the fingers of a hand, as in horse chestnut leaves.

*The leaves of **nettles** are **simple** and coarsely toothed. Rowan, on the other hand, gives an example of **compound** leaves - in this case there are nine pairs of finely-toothed leaflets, with a terminal leaflet at the end.*

Relation to stem. The leaves might be all in a rosette at ground level, as in a daisy. They could be in whorls up the stem as in cleavers. If the leaves are in pairs, they can be opposite each other, or alternately up the stem. The chief possibilities here are shown below.

Different arrangements of leaves: *basal rosette, whorled, opposite, alternate*

*Stitchworts (right), like virtually all the members of the Pink family, have pairs of leaves **opposite** each other. Burdock (above), by contrast, has **alternate** leaves.*

Stem

What could possibly be interesting about the stem? Well, in some cases this might be your best clue for separating several very similar species. In St John's worts, for example, the stems come in round, square, ridged, hairy, smooth, red, green and various combinations of these characters.

Examine the stem (preferably through your lens) and run your fingers over it gently. Is it woody or herbaceous? Stiff or pliant? Robust or delicate? Is it round, square, ridged, winged? Is it smooth, rough, downy, hairy, bristly, sticky? Examine the whole stem, as the top is sometimes different from the base. Make notes on all the features of the stem that you can detect.

*Although without flowers, this plant can be identified as a St John's wort by the design and arrangement of the leaves. Even from a photograph, the **square red stem** suggests it is the aptly named square-stalked St John's wort.*

Texture

Apart from a few unusual features, the main aspect of texture is **hairiness**. We have seen that a hairy stem may give you an ID clue. Many other parts of the plant may have varying degrees and types of hairiness. Hairy flower stalks or hairy sepals may be noteworthy. If the leaves are hairy, check whether it is on the upper side or the underside or both. Even flowers occasionally sport hairs on the petals.

The hairs themselves can range from soft and downy to stiff and prickly. Hairs can be long or short, dense or scanty (the latter being termed 'pubescent' - delightfully suggestive of adolescent cheeks). They may stick out from the stem or be closely pressed to it; they may be simple or branched. 'Glandular hairs' sound as though they might have a nasty disease, but if you look through your lens at a plant that is described as having glandular hairs, you will see that some or all hairs have a tiny droplet of moisture at the tip. These may give the plant a sticky feel when you handle it; they may even release a scent when rubbed.

*These hips of Japanese rose (a garden escape) show **glandular hairs** on the sepals, fruits and pedicels. The tiny drops of moisture tipping the hairs often result in a sticky or aromatic plant.*

PROTECTION RACKETS

In some ways, plants solicit the attention of birds, bugs and so on. Insects are attracted by various methods, such as providing nectar, so that they will inadvertently spread pollen between the flowers they visit. Later on in the plant's lifecycle, birds and animals become more important: it's the fruit that entices them, so - again inadvertently - seeds are transported to new homes when the animal or bird discards, buries or excretes them.

In many other respects, however, plants need to keep animals at arm's length, since chewed leaves, swallowed flowers and trampled stems constitute injury to the plant, threatening its chances of survival and reproduction. One way in which plants protect themselves from attack is by growing close to the ground, with leaves in a basal rosette. But some have more dramatic defences.

*Not for nothing is this called the **spear thistle** - grazing animals are unlikely to risk lacerating their mouths on its spines.*

Thorns, spines and prickles are modified leaves, twigs or hairs. They deter animals which have dining designs on the plant. Downward-pointing (recurved) prickles as on some roses hinder small creatures which may try to climb up the stems. A mat of hairs on a leaf makes it harder for a caterpillar or bug to chew. The hairs of stinging nettles inject a chemical into the skin; humans and other animals soon learn to avoid them. Other toxins are released when parts of certain plants are chewed. Alkaloids are responsible for the bitter, off-putting taste of some buttercups and poppies, for example, and also of the hemlock famously drunk by Socrates. It is not yet well understood why tomatoes are perfectly edible to humans, while deadly nightshade berries - both members of the very same *Solanum* genus - are precisely the opposite.

Scent

A sense of smell is rather an idiosyncratic thing; some people think meadowsweet has a luscious smell, for instance, while others consider it horribly sickly-sweet. The human nose is said to be able to distinguish 10,000 different scents. But alertness to scents - nice or nasty - can be helpful in the business of ID. Each member of the mint group, for example, has its own distinctive scent - peppermint, spearmint and so on. The strong garlicky smell of ramsons being trampled underfoot is often what first alerts you to its presence - a pleasure or pain depending on whether or not you like garlic!

*Meadowsweet (right) and ramsons (above) have very different **scents**: the first rather cloyingly sweet, the second strongly garlicky.*

You can educate your sense of smell by constant use. What's more, some flowers and leaves just smell heavenly so why not enjoy them? Examples you may find rewarding are fragrant orchid, thyme, bog myrtle, feverfew and many more. One of my favourites is creeping thistle, perhaps because somehow one doesn't expect what many regard as a troublesome weed to have such a pleasant scent.

Experienced field botanists occasionally even taste part of a plant to support an ID, especially if flowers are lacking. The taste of water-pepper, for example, is just what it says on the tin.

Fruit

In the case of some families such as the Crucifers, it is often necessary to examine the fruit to get down to species level. (Note: **'family'** has a particular meaning in botany, which is discussed on page 90. In this book, the only English names capitalised are those of botanical families. The Crucifers are also known as the Cabbage family.) Look around and see if any of the plants are far enough on to have produced fruits. You might even want to come back later in the year if you are really keen to clinch an identification. There will be more about fruits later in this chapter.

Habit

The habit of a plant is how it grows and what form it takes. We have already distinguished the herb

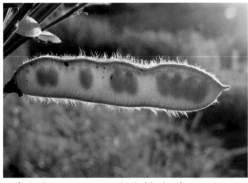

*Its **fruit** demonstrates unmistakably that **broom** is a member of the Pea family.*

habit (dying back every year) from the tree or shrub habit. Most herbs grow upright - what the books call 'erect'.

Another kind of growth form is the **creeping** or **prostrate** habit. This means growing along the ground instead of upright. Mountain and coastal plants often adopt this habit because they gain protection from the elements by keeping close to ground level. Where plants are grazed by animals they may have a prostrate habit - like some clovers - to minimise their chances of being eaten. Plants like this usually put down roots at intervals as they grow. Keep an eye on creeping buttercups for a while at the edge of a path or other bare area: as every gardener knows, it doesn't take them long to get roots down as they steadily encroach on the virgin territory.

***Bindweed** can be a spectacular climber, reaching ever upwards on a natural or man-made support, as here; or spreading sideways over surrounding vegetation.*

Another possible habit is to use nearby plants as a framework for growth by climbing up them or twining round them. The **climbers** and **scramblers**, such as bindweeds and vetches are likely to have rather weak, pliable stems of their own and may have tendrils for attaching themselves to other plants.

A few plants such as broomrapes are genuinely **parasitic**. They don't just grow on other plants, they actually derive their nourishment from their hosts. Others are semi-parasitic, only flourishing in the presence of particular companions.

Jizz

Jizz is a word that birdwatchers have used for a long time, but botanists have more recently discovered what a useful term it is. The **jizz** of a plant is what makes it instantly recognisable from a brief glimpse. It's what makes the passenger-botanist cry 'Stop!' to their long-suffering partner who is driving, when they spot

*What tells you from a distance that you are looking at a mass of bluebells? The habitat (woodland), the colour (that particular slightly purplish blue), the habit (a level sheet of flowerheads), even the smell: these all add up to bluebell **jizz**.*

a wayside plant they really yearn to take a closer look at. Sometimes it's just the colour; for example, the scarlet of a common poppy is unmistakable. Or it could be the sheer size: giant hogweed, anyone? More often it's a subtle blend of colour, size, habit, habitat and so on which simply has the name of the plant written all over it.

Obviously, the more practice you have, the more familiar the jizz of various plants will become, so you might try a little experimenting as to which plants you already instinctively know by their jizz. Can you spot a rose at a hundred paces? Or bluebells at 40 mph? Could that bank of tall mauve spikes be anything but rosebay willowherb? Ask yourself what caught your eye and gave you the answer almost before your brain could register the details.

*Another plant with an unmistakable jizz - the **yellow iris** or **flag**.*

PLANTS IN MOTION

We imagine that, unlike birds and animals, plants keep still, but do they? Insect-eating plants certainly don't. Britain boasts several insectivorous plants, such as the sundews and butterworts. These plants live in soils which are very low in nutrients, especially nitrogen, so they have evolved the ability to obtain nutrients from insects instead. To this

Sundews (this is round-leaved, the most common sundew) trap insects for food by means of the sticky glands on their leaves.

end, they have various mechanisms such as sticky leaves to ensnare their insect food. In some cases, the leaves curl up once the insect is trapped. In other species such as the bladderworts, a kind of sucking mechanism prevents insects from escaping. Pitcher plants are found naturalised in a few places in Britain; they have a water-filled trap in which insects drown.

In our time-frame, **brambles** appear motionless, but time-lapse photography shows them riding roughshod over the surrounding vegetation, weaving an all-but-impenetrable jungle of thorny tentacles.

Sunflowers - *these are being cultivated as a crop - turn their heads so that they are constantly facing the sun.*

Another way that plants can be said to move is if you view them in a different time-frame, such as is seen in time-lapse photography. Everyone who has seen clips from David Attenborough's television series 'The Life of Plants' will surely remember the brambles. When hours of growth were compressed into mere seconds, brambles appeared sinisterly purposeful as they crept and clambered through the undergrowth, using any nearby plant as a temporary anchor to get them to the next place.

Quite a few plants also move by turning towards the light of the sun as it travels across the sky, while others respond to the sun by opening and closing at different times of day. In Victorian times, there was a fashion for planting beds with species that favour different opening times, so that the whole bed could be viewed as a clock. Goatsbeard is sometimes known as Jack-go-to-bed-at-noon, because of its habit of closing promptly at midday. Evening primroses open at dusk, just as scarlet pimpernels are closing for the night. And of course the name 'daisy' is simply a contraction of 'day's eye.'

Assembling the evidence

You now have quite a lot to study and to ponder when trying to identify a particular plant. So start practising, because in botanising that's definitely what makes perfect (well, better, anyway). Study a plant growing wild (even if it's just a weed in your garden) and note your judgement on all the characters we have looked at. Besides the flower itself, we can now add notes about all the other features we have examined:

- plant size
- leaf design and arrangement
- stem
- hairiness
- scent
- fruit, if available
- habit

Yellow rattle, *showing the calyx (sepals), below the lipped flower, inflated when the fruit is forming. If you shake it when the seeds have hardened, you can hear them rattle. This plant is often known as* **hay rattle** *because the seed becoming ripe used to be taken as a sign to begin hay-making.*

A prickly purple composite - what can it be but a **thistle**? *That only leaves you with a choice from about fifteen thistle species . . . (This picture is in fact of creeping thistle.)*

Suppose my notes told me that

- the (dicot) flowers are purple and composite
- the plant is medium to tall in height
- the leaves are simple, not compound, but deeply toothed and spiny
- the stem is prickly
- the fruit is feathery.

Yes, it's a thistle (though precisely which thistle is not established yet). And you may have equally little difficulty identifying your own specimen. But thistles are fairly catholic in their choice of places to grow - fields, hedgerows, waste ground and so on, all over the country. In contrast, some plants are restricted to specialised places, or habitats, which is the subject of the next chapter. Before that, however, we shall take a look at the life story of a plant.

THE LIFE STORY OF A PLANT

Life cycle

As we have seen, the flower is only one aspect of a flowering plant, albeit the most vital of all, since it is the sexual apparatus that results in the formation of seed for the next generation. Before it gets to this stage, however, the plant has to set up shop. That is, it must establish a root system both to anchor it in the ground and to provide a way of obtaining nutrients and water it needs from the soil. Next it needs a stem to raise it above ground level so that the leaves can soak up the sun, the insects can reach the pollen and future seeds have a chance to distance themselves from the parent plant. Then comes the flower, attracting pollinators to facilitate sex-at-a-distance. Finally the fruit forms and the seeds are dispersed. If conditions are suitable the seeds germinate, starting the process all over again. The diagram below explains how the life cycle works.

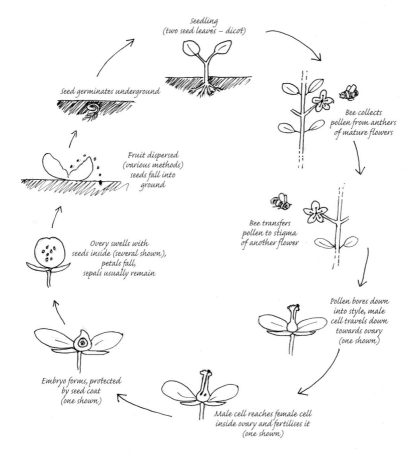

Seedling
(two seed leaves – dicot)

Seed germinates underground

Bee collects
pollen from anthers
of mature flowers

Fruit dispersed
(various methods)
seeds fall into
ground

Bee transfers
pollen to stigma
of another flower

Ovary swells with
seeds inside (several shown),
petals fall,
sepals usually remain

Pollen bores down
into style, male
cell travels down
towards ovary
(one shown)

Embryo forms, protected
by seed coat
(one shown)

Male cell reaches female cell
inside ovary and fertilises it
(one shown)

LIFE CYCLE OF A FLOWERING PLANT

In the case of some plant families, studying the **fruit** may have an important role to play in identification. But what exactly is a fruit? There is an old argument about whether a tomato is a fruit or a vegetable, but this is merely a culinary quibble: a tomato is undeniably a fruit, but cooks use it in ways that usually apply to vegetables. To a botanist, the fruit is simply the ripened ovary containing the seeds. The fruit is often palatable to birds and animals, so they have an incentive to eat it. Thus they disperse the seeds - which pass unharmed through the digestive system - elsewhere. (Tomato plants are occasionally found at picnic sites - but it's not what you're thinking! They have grown from seeds that drop out of sandwiches.)

Fruits may be large or small, from pineapples to cherries. They can be fleshy like plums, or hard like nuts. The seeds can be on the inside of the fruit - as

in tomatoes - or on the outside, as in strawberries. They can be round and simple, designed just to fall to the ground and be eaten or rotted down to expose the seeds. Or they may have useful appendages like the wings of sycamore seeds, or the feathery bits making up a dandelion's 'clock', so that they can easily be wafted away by the wind. So in a botanical sense, tomatoes are definitely fruits, as are many other 'vegetables'. Carrots, on the other hand, are modified roots and cabbages are modified leaves.

Two very different structures, yet both are **fruits: dandelion** *pappus (top) and (bottom) the berries of a garden variety of* **rowan**.

WHICH PART OF THE PLANT?
We have settled the argument that a tomato is indeed a fruit, not a vegetable. But can you say which part of the plant is responsible for various household consumables? From which part of the plant in question do the following come - root, leaf, stem or what?
Rhubarb, brussels sprouts, cauliflower, garlic, mangetout, asparagus, rice, saffron, tapioca, artichoke, angelica, cinnamon, maple syrup.
(Answers on page 58.)

Annuals and perennials

Annuals run through their complete life cycle in a single season. They grow from seed, produce leaves and flowers, bear fruit, wither and die, all between, say, April and September. The seeds they produce are scattered nearby or carried away by birds or by wind or water, or perhaps stuck to animal coats in the form of burs, and the process starts all over again. This may be just next door to their parents, or somewhere else entirely.

Burdock fruits are well-known for sticking to clothing and to animals' coats - a means of transporting the fruits away from the parent plant.

Silverweed *spreads rapidly by means of **stolons**, prostrate stems which reach out over the ground, putting down roots every few inches.*

Perennials, on the other hand, are relatively permanent features of their situation. When they have set seed, they 'die back' but not in a permanent pushing-up-the-daisies sense. Their underground parts (roots, bulbs, etc.) live on to start up again the following year. Sometimes above-ground parts such as leaves carry on through the winter too, in which case they are known as winter-green species.

Whereas annuals are almost entirely dependent on seeds to provide the next generation, perennials can get along for quite a while without producing viable seeds (or when those seeds fall upon stony ground, as it were) since the whole plant is likely to survive anyway. Another method of propagating themselves is to have roots or runners which send up new shoots at intervals, eventually becoming independent of the original plant.

Biennials are a halfway house. In their first year from seed, they concentrate on getting roots established and producing leaves to absorb the sunlight necessary for continued growth and production. This often results in their showing a basal rosette of leaves throughout the first season. Come the second year, they produce their flowers and fruits. Only then do they die completely. There are not nearly so many biennial species as annuals and perennials - it's quite a specialised way of life.

I remember feeling very frustrated when I started to botanise in earnest, because the first thing in the handbook description was so often 'annual' or 'perennial'. While I had a rough idea what the words meant (in gardening terms at least) I had no idea at all how I was supposed to decide which applied. Was I meant to wait all year to see if it came up again in the same place? Take seeds from it and plant them? Maybe I should mark the spot and then dig it up during the winter to see if the plant was still there (which, of course, it wouldn't be after I'd finished doing that). Or perhaps the implication was that I should try uprooting it to see how valiantly it resisted. But wasn't there something about it being a criminal offence to uproot a plant in the wild?

Perhaps the methods suggested above are the only sure-fire ways to tell an annual from a perennial, but there are a few clues that will give an indication. Because they only have to last out the season, the stems of annuals are often fairly weak; plants have to be very careful about how they invest their limited resources - they don't waste them on things they don't need. But this is not an inflexible rule: it might be more important to the plant that it can stand up to competition or to the weather, so it could be worth spending some resources on a strong stem. However, if your specimen has a strong stem, is well-rooted in the ground and you can see non-flowering shoots nearby (i.e. green parts only) as well as flowering shoots, it is very likely to be perennial. But if you only meant to pluck the flower and the whole plant comes up in your hand, roots and all (whoops!) it's probably an annual.

Nipplewort is an **annual** plant, which can grow quite tall, up to about 1 m, but it is rather weak and tends to borrow a bit of support from other plants, or in this case from a wall.

Seasons

Knowing the time of year when a plant is likely to be in flower can be a good aid to identification, and most fieldguides provide this information. In a mild winter, some stalwarts such as daisies, groundsel, chickweed and shepherd's purse may be found in flower right through the year. Most, however, have a regular place in the seasonal succession, which varies little from year to year. Country lanes often seem to be continuously decorated with lacy white umbellifers: not everyone realises, though, that which white umbellifer depends on when you are looking - cow parsley in April, hogweed in May, ground elder in June and hedge parsley in July is a common sequence. It's a similar story among the heathers on the moors: bell heather (the deepest purple) comes first in May, then cross-leaved heath (deep pink) in June, joined finally by ling (pinkish purple) in July. Both these sequences may be up to a month later, however, depending on how far north you are.

Waiting for the first wild flowers to appear in spring is a pleasant anticipation. Some people are inclined to exclaim 'Oh, look, snowdrops - spring is on its way!' However, apparently 'wild' snowdrops are almost always garden escapes, or even deliberately planted, and many weeks - and much snow, ice, frost and other unspringlike weather - may pass between the first snowdrops and the first genuine harbingers of spring. Better candidates for 'first flowers' might be coltsfoot, lesser celandine, barren strawberry or butterbur, depending on the weather conditions. Some plants require a period of frost before they start up for the season, whereas others prefer milder weather and earlier sunshine.

*A **lacy white umbellifer** beside a path - but which one is it? Detective work suggests the solution: the grass is well grown, yet some of the trees are not in leaf yet. This indicates April or early May (if further north) so **cow parsley** is the likely answer, confirmed by the leaf design and the fruits which are just starting to form.*

Coltsfoot flowers *have a habit of sprouting suddenly from a brown winter background while your back is turned, in February or early March (depending on latitude and weather conditions). The leaves appear later, after the flowers are finished.*

Because of this, the order in which plants begin to flower varies more in early spring than in other seasons. Flowering season is not always a reliable character, however; primroses, for example - whose very name means 'first rose' - can occasionally be found flowering in late autumn.

Origins and extinctions

Hybrids. In the animal world, hybridisation is very rare in the wild and evolutionary

At the top of the picture is the darker purple **bell heather***, at the bottom, the pale purple* **ling***; in the centre just a few flowers of* **cross-leaved heath** *are still pink - the rest have withered ('gone over') by the time the ling starts to flower, and show here as light brown. This photograph was taken in early September in Scotland.*

pressures will usually make short work of any that do crop up. Deliberate human intervention was needed to produce the zeedonk, beefalo and tigon, for example; the spontaneous creation of totally new animals is unheard of. But plants are rather different. Because of the way they handle chromosomes plants can and do hybridise, in many cases quite freely; from time to time even completely new species are occasionally thrown up. Unlike zoos, botanic gardens - and even common-or-garden gardens - are full of hybrids. The same is true to a lesser extent of plants in the wild. Occasionally hybrids are not just between closely related species of the same genus, but even between species from different genera (see page 90 for an explanation of these terms).

Once you begin to get the hang of the common species themselves, the presence of hybrids in the wild makes botanising all the more tantalising. Orchids - some of the most recently evolved of plants - are especially given to variation, occasionally coming up with something the experts agree is to be looked upon as a new species.

A BRAND NEW PLANT

Once upon a time, there was a native grass called small cord-grass or *Spartina maritima*. (*Spartina* is from the Greek word for a rope or cord, *maritima* means 'growing by the sea'. For more about scientific names, see page 94.) Then, in the 19th century, another cord-grass called *Spartina alterniflora* was accidentally introduced from North America, probably in ships' ballast. These two species interbred, and from their hybrid there arose a new, fully fertile species, which was named *Spartina anglica*.

The new species turned out to be very vigorous and fast-growing, which led to the bright idea of planting it to stabilise the soil on mudflats in many parts of Britain (and as far abroad as China). Unfortunately, *Spartina anglica* went over the top: of its own accord it colonised many areas important to wintering wildfowl and waders for food and shelter. One place badly affected was the National Nature Reserve at Lindisfarne. Eventually the problem here was solved by 'rotoburying' - ploughing the roots deep underground until they suffocated. However, the new species may also have caused the loss of the native cord-grass from many areas. Like the aliens discussed on page 11, new plants may have both benefits and drawbacks.

Spartina anglica or **common cord grass** arose spontaneously in Southampton Water in about 1890. It has the power to spread rapidly over mudflats, stabilising the ground, yet likely to crowd out other species that get in its way.

Extinctions. Extinctions are a different matter. As a loss of individuality and a loss to diversity, they are always something of a tragedy that perhaps could have been prevented. Extinctions may be at a local level ('extirpations') - no longer in Devon, say, but still in Cornwall. In such cases, there may be a move among conservationists to 'translocate' some plants from Cornwall back to a former site in Devon. However, if the same factors are at work, it may not thrive when reintroduced unless tended with extra special care. If a plant is widely distributed in northern Europe, then its disappearance from the British flora is much lamented, but at least it still exists somewhere. If, however, the plant is endemic to Britain - that is to say, it does not grow anywhere else in the world - then it is irreplaceable.

*Alpine butterwort is now extinct in the British Isles, but you may see **pale butterwort** in an acid bog, most likely in the far north-west of Scotland.*

Why do wild plants go extinct? In the Victorian and Edwardian eras especially, the commonest reason was collection. Rare herbs, ferns and so on were hunted down and dug up to glorify a keen botanist's garden, herbarium (collection of pressed specimens) or ironically-named conservatory. Sooner or later (and unrecognised by the agent of its downfall) the very last wild specimen was dug up. Mere picking of flowers may also tip a plant over the edge into extinction, since the flower loses its chance to produce seeds so regeneration may never take place. This is why the Code of Conduct (see page 130) stresses not to pick flowers unless very plentiful.

LOST TO BRITAIN

The alpine butterwort was first discovered in Britain on the Black Isle in eastern Scotland in 1831. This is a beautiful white-flowered plant of mountainous regions, with a rosette of often reddish leaves. As in other butterworts, the leaves are covered in sticky glands by which insects are trapped and subsequently 'eaten' by the plant, in compensation for the lack of nitrogen in boggy soil. The site on the Black Isle was its only confirmed location in the British Isles, though the plant is found in northern Eurasia from Finland to the Himalayas. Botanists came from far and wide to pay their respects but alas, quite a few took some home for their collections. In addition, cultivation encroached, the soil began to dry out, and one day the alpine butterwort as a British native was no more. The last specimen was seen there in 1919.

Angelica *is best known for its candied stems, used in cake decoration. However, the leaves, roots and seeds are also used in various schools of folk medicine.*

As the twentieth century progressed, pollution and loss of habitat became more insidious factors, as more wild places were tamed for agriculture, built on for housing, or subjected to pressure from nearby roads, industrial sites and so on. As the new millennium approached, the threat of global warming reared its head. Climate determines temperature, rainfall and wind, not to mention sea level. So climate change implies habitat change and habitat change results in the loss of some species that can live nowhere else. On the positive side, new - perhaps warmer and wetter - habitats may encourage species from elsewhere to settle here of their own accord.

ANSWERS TO QUIZ (page 51)

RHUBARB - leaf stalk   BRUSSELS SPROUTS - leaf buds

CAULIFLOWER - flower   GARLIC - bulb

MANGETOUT - fruit   ASPARAGUS - stem

RICE - fruit or seed, depending on whether it's husked

SAFFRON - stigma   TAPIOCA - root

ARTICHOKE - flower bud   ANGELICA - stem

CINNAMON - bark   MAPLE SYRUP - sap

WHERE TO LOOK

Why do different plants grow in different places? Some answers to this question are the subject of this chapter.

There are very few places, even in inner cities, where wild plants do not grow. Wherever you live, you shouldn't have to go far to find a place to botanise. Your local area is always a good place to start because you can return at will. For example, if you didn't have a reference book with you at first, you can bring one the next time - or maybe summon a second opinion to the spot. If an interesting-looking specimen wasn't quite in flower, you can return when it is. Or if it is one of those tricky Crucifers, you might want to come back a bit later in the year to examine the fruits. On a longer timescale, you may care to monitor locations or populations from year to year.

When you have more time to spare - at the weekend or on holiday, say - you can plan a more focussed excursion. If you know you are going to the coast, for example, why not read up on coastal plants beforehand so that you have an idea what to look for? The same goes for a holiday in a mountain region. Perhaps you live most of the year in a chalk area of south-east England? You could plan a holiday in a location that's completely different such as the Highlands of Scotland (remembering, of course, to devise persuasive arguments as to why it will be just perfect for the rest of the family).

WHAT PLANTS NEED

If you think about it, you will realise that you already know something about the needs of plants, if you've spent any time at all in natural surroundings. You know perfectly well that you are not going to find poppies on top of a mountain, for example; that it would be futile to look for bluebells on a shingle beach, and that daisies don't grow in ponds. In other words, these are mismatches between a plant and its **habitat**.

Poppies *may flourish by the shore in suitable conditions but, being by nature arable weeds, they are never going to be found on mountain tops (not until the climate changes out of all recognition, anyway).*

The natural habitat of a plant is the kind of place it prefers to grow in. Gardeners manipulate various conditions such as moisture, shade or acidity level, so as to favour the plants they want to grow. Under natural conditions, however, the plants do the choosing. The ones we know as 'weeds' are usually not very fussy about where they live, but others have such special requirements that there is only one type of habitat in which they will settle.

A good way to get to grips with habitat is to see it in terms of a set of conditions or parameters which in combination make up a certain type of mini-environment. The main parameters are:

- moisture
- sunlight
- soil
- altitude
- disturbance.

Moisture

This refers to how wet or dry the soil conditions are. This in turn depends on (a) how high the rainfall is, (b) how good the drainage is, and (c) how fast the surface water can be evaporated by sun and wind. An area may be damp or boggy because it gets a lot of rain, because it is poorly drained, because little evaporation takes place - or a combination of all three. Dry soil may be well-drained (for example, sandy soil drains readily) and/or in a sunny spot and/or in an area of low rainfall.

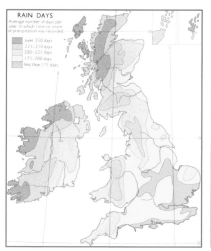

The number of rainy days across the British Isles

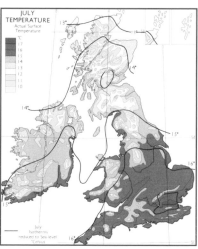

July temperatures

Sunlight

Most people are aware that the east of Britain has more sunny days than the west, and that the south is warmer than the north. But equally important from the plant's point of view is the availability of sunlight in its immediate vicinity. If it lives under beech trees (which are one of the shadiest of all deciduous trees) it doesn't matter how long the sun blazes from a clear blue sky - the plant won't

Wood anemones may flourish even in the deep shade of a beechwood.

be getting the full benefit. The air will be warm, of course, but plants use the sunlight itself in order to photosynthesise and produce some of the nutrients they need for growth - you could almost say that plants 'eat sunshine'. So wooded areas favour plants that can get by with less direct sunlight. The flipside is that woods are sheltered places, so plants in woodland are protected from wind, from the immediate effects of a downpour and to some extent from frost as well.

Soil

One thing to notice about soil is whether it is deep or shallow. Thin soil, down to virtually none at all, is what some plants - such as the ones you grow on your rockery - like best. They have roots which are shallow but very hard-working, clinging fast to rocks or digging themselves among stones, and extracting all possible nutrients from the limited supply. At the other end of the scale are plants with deep roots that need deep soil to tap into. Thin soil will be found on rocky surfaces, higher up on mountains, in sandy areas and so on. Deep soils are quite often damp, as in water meadows, woodland and peat bogs.

Here **English stonecrop** has found a tiny quantity of soil deep down between boulders, from which it can spread over the face of the rocks.

The other important point is the **acidity** of the soil. If chemistry was not your golden subject at school, you may feel rather anxious about trying to understand acidity and the mysteries of pH. All you have to grasp in this context, however, is that acidity levels are very important to most plants. Soils that are strongly alkaline (**basic** soils, as they are usually called in botanical circles) support a suite or 'community' of plants quite different from those found in acid soils and - with few exceptions - never the twain shall meet. Alkaline soils in this country are mainly those formed from chalk and limestone rocks. Acid soils are lacking in the calcium supplied by those rocks. Neutral soils, which are usually clayey, fall somewhere between the two extremes. As for pH, you only need remember that pH6 is acidic, pH7 is neutral and pH8 is alkaline - not many plants are interested in soil that falls outside these limits.

Altitude

Although some of our plants - the 'alpines', for example - are apparently only found on mountains, this is not always a matter of absolute height above sea level. Reasons for plants doing well in mountainous regions include:

- left high and dry by the ice ages and been there ever since

- so bothered by competition that will only flourish where others can't

- prefer a cooler atmosphere, so may be found at sea level further north

- like, or at least tolerate, stony and rocky conditions

- have the ability to crouch close to the ground, out of the worst of the weather.

Alpine fleabane *is not only a mountain specialist, but a basic-soil specialist. In Britain it is found in a few limestone mountain areas, on crags where sheep and deer cannot reach it. These sites are at the southern limit of this arctic plant, its strongholds being in such places as Greenland and Siberia.*

MOUNTAIN DISCOVERIES

It is often supposed that nineteenth century poets and painters such as Wordsworth and Turner were the first people to recognise that there was beauty to be found in wild and lonely places. Certainly, in mediaeval times mountains were regarded as god-forsaken, sinister and dangerous places with no redeeming features. However, it was earlier botanists who actually presaged the view of wilderness as beautiful and romantic. The great seventeenth century botanist John Ray argued that besides being the source of pure water that flowed down in streams and burns, mountains were 'very ornamental to the earth, affording pleasant and delightful prospects.'. In 1661, Ray was the first to record the yellow mountain saxifrage from Westmorland, and in 1668 he found purple saxifrage on Ingleborough. Even earlier, the botanist Thomas Johnson had discovered starry saxifrage and alpine saxifrage on Snowdon in 1639. Thus botanists opened up the glory of mountains and the flowers belonging to them which grace so many lowland rock gardens today.

Disturbance

As every gardener knows, ground that is dug up and then left to itself will very shortly be found to be hosting a quantity of various 'weeds'. Some will have come from seeds in the **seedbank** - that is to say, they were in the soil all along but didn't have a chance to get going until now. (Some seeds can live for decades, even centuries, while waiting for the right opportunity.) Other seeds may have been dropped by birds, blown in by the wind, or accidentally transferred from places nearby. What they all have in common is their ability to make hay while the sun shines. They are usually annuals which grow, flower, produce the next generation's seeds, then wither and die, all in a single season.

If disturbances persist - if the ground is dug up, harrowed, trampled by people or animals, compressed by vehicles, and so on - then such seeds as have set will have to grow again from scratch next year - though probably in different spots, in different proportions and with different neighbours.

In contrast, if the disturbance is a one-off occurrence then, as time goes on, the comparatively weak annuals will be overtaken in the race for space by more robust, longer-lived plants that gradually get a foothold. Perennials live on in reduced circumstances over the winter, so a pattern of plants will begin to emerge. Left alone, the wasteland may be gradually transformed into a more settled habitat, until

Pineappleweed, *a well-established alien annual, is a common find on* **disturbed ground**. *Squeeze it between your fingers - it really does smell of pineapple.*

sooner or later it no longer counts as 'disturbed ground'.

Although disturbed ground is a habitat in its own right, it is impossible to make a definitive list of plants that grow there, as they may be anything from arable weeds - poppies, fumitories, cornflowers (if you're very lucky) and others that team up with farmed crops - to opportunistic aliens. Bittercresses and willowherbs are other typical plants of disturbed ground.

HABITATS

Various combinations of the conditions listed above produce different recognisable habitat types. The National Vegetation Classification scheme currently distinguishes 286 such 'communities'. However, we will content ourselves with just five major groups: woodland, grassland, bogs and fens, heathlands and coastal.

Woodland

'Woodland' isn't just virgin forest, but includes shady places in general, such as riverbanks and hedgerows with shrubs and trees, shelter belts and so on. Places that were once wooded but have now been cleared often show many of the floristic characteristics of woodland. Woods may be damp - often called 'carr' - or dry; they may be high or low, acidic or alkaline according to parent rock. What they have in common is that when the trees are in leaf, little sunlight reaches the plants on the ground. So woodland plants tend either to flower early in the year, before the canopy closes over, or to be more tolerant of shade than the tall grasses which would overwhelm them outside the cover of the trees. Most plants will be perennials: it's not an easy place for opportunists to find an opening.

*One of our prettiest **woodland flowers** does not, to my mind, have one of the prettiest names: **chickweed wintergreen**. It is unusual in having between five and nine petals, with a whorl below the single flower often containing a matching number of leaves.*

Typical woodland plants are primroses, bluebells, dog's mercury, enchanter's nightshade and the appropriately named wood sorrel and wood anemone. Umbellifers are a particular feature of hedgerows.

__Leopard's-bane__ is a garden escape, and a rather attractive one, although it does tend to take over large areas of shady hedgerow and woodland corners.

Grassland

Much of the grassland we see in the countryside is 'improved'; that is to say, farmers have managed it intensively over many years, by fertilising, reseeding and so on, to improve the grazing for animals and the quality of hay made from the grass. The pH is likely to be around 7 (neutral). Natural chalk and limestone grasslands may be pH8 or even higher. Chalk and limestone grasslands generally have a rich flora with many different plants flowering throughout a long season. However, they are often in areas much sought after for other purposes and conservationists need to be ever alert to such threats. Plants that favour basic soils are known to botanists as **calcicoles** whereas those that avoid basic soils are called **calcifuges**.

*A low-growing plant with delicate tissue-like petals, the **common rockrose**, is mainly confined to chalk and limestone grasslands.*

Orchids are often the pride of chalk and limestone sites while gentians, rockroses and rarer violets are other specialities. Traveller's joy in a hedgerow is a very good indicator of basic soil.

Bogs and fens

There are many names for soggy places, such as mire, marsh, moss and swamp. The two most used in botanical parlance are bog and fen. These are generally understood to mean 'acid soggy place' and 'base-rich (alkaline) soggy place' respectively.

In **bogs**, acid conditions arise because the soil consists mainly of an accumulation of slowly decaying organic matter, usually resulting in peat formation. This is a habitat which is nutritionally very poor. The dominant plants tend to be sphagnum mosses and sedges, with shrubs such as heather and broom on the drier sections, but some orchids also appreciate boggy conditions. Because of the low level of nutrients, a few flowering plants such as sundews and butterworts are insectivorous, that is, they trap insects to supplement their diet.

*The leaves of **common butterwort** are shown here with flies glued to the sticky glands which cover the leaves.*

While bogs receive their moisture mainly from rainfall, **fens** receive more from water flowing through calcareous (chalk and limestone) soils. This provides them with a much higher level of nutrition, with the result that grasses and sedges are more abundant and there is a richer flora in general. Plants you are likely to see here are meadowsweet, marsh marigold, ragged robin and valerian. Fens need careful management, however, or they are liable to be taken over by shrubs and eventually by trees in the course of natural succession.

Heathlands

Heaths are usually acid habitats, which can occur either on lowland sandy soils or on the drier parts of moorland where they are mixed with or grade into peat bogs. Like bogs, heathlands have a much restricted flora because of low nutrient levels and, in the case of

*The flowers of two **heathland shrubs, gorse** and **broom**, look rather similar. Gorse (left) is the spiny one, while broom (right) has no spines, but distinctive trefoil leaves.*

sandy heaths, low moisture levels as well since sand drains so readily.

Gorse (known as furze or whin in different parts of the country), bilberry and heather are the mainstays of heath vegetation. These are shrubs with woody stems - though sometimes quite small and with very attractive flowers;

heaths support few true herbs. However, if you are lucky enough to be gazing out over an area dotted liberally with heath spotted orchids in countless subtle shades, you may feel that a heath is a delightfully flowery place.

Coastal

Salt is toxic to most plants, so those that grow near the sea need to be tolerant of the salt that may be splashed onto them by waves or carried by the inshore breezes. In addition, the soil may be very poor and thin in such places as sand dunes, shingle or rocky cliffs. However, where sand is formed by ground-down shells rather than from minerals, it will be basic rather than acid because shells are rich in calcium carbonate. This type of sandy soil will support a richer flora, just as basic grasslands are richer than acid ones. One of the most interesting facets of coastal vegetation is the zoning that occurs at increasing distances from the sea. Some plants are found right at the edge, even periodically covered by salt water or constantly steeped in it on a saltmarsh. Others are more fussy about getting too much salt and live further up the shore. Yet others may shelter in at the base of the cliffs or perch precariously higher up.

Thrift: one of the commonest of seashore plants (though it may also occasionally be found inland).

Sea spurreys have some of the prettiest flowers to be found on saltmarshes, where they are often accompanied by thrift, sea aster and scurvygrass. The latter is not a grass at all but a succulent herb with white flowers.

Roseroot (the crushed roots give off a scent of roses) is a **succulent** plant: its leaves store fresh water, of which there may not be a regular supply in the habitat. This plant is often found on sea cliffs, and also inland on mountain ledges.

Succulent plants have fleshy leaves and/or stems in which to store fresh water for a non-rainy day (as it were). Besides being found on the coast, they are common in deserts in other countries (cacti) and other places with a poor water supply. In this country, members of the stonecrop group (see picture on page 62), found in stony and rocky places, are usually succulent.

SHORE ZONES

Which plants you will find on the seashore depends firstly on whether the shore is rocky, sandy, shingle or mud (saltmarsh), as these are distinct habitats in their own right. However, sandbanks often provide the clearest evidence of zoning.

The only flowering plants which grow actually in the sea are the eel-grasses and tasselweeds (*Zostera* and *Ruppia* species). Along the drift line, between the sea and the dunes, you may discover saltwort, sea rocket or sea sandwort. Further back from the water's edge, couch, marram and other grasses with long roots are starting to stabilise the dunes. They may be accompanied by sea bindweed, burnet rose, sea holly and other plants which can cope with the shifting sands. Further back again, where the dunes have become fixed,

Wild thyme is a common plant of stable dunes, but is also found all over the British Isles on grasslands and heaths. The leaves have a very distinctive scent.

you may find birdsfoot trefoil, stork's-bill and thyme, which are not restricted to coastal habitats. In the damp hollows known as dune slacks the flora can be excitingly rich, and you may be lucky enough to see marsh or fen orchids.

You can see from the above account that interesting plants may be found just about anywhere but exactly which collection of plants you will see depends on the nature of the habitat. There is another factor, though, in what plants to expect where: the restraints of geography. This is what we shall examine in the next section.

Dune slacks are the damp hollows between sand dunes. They are often much richer in flowers than the ridges.

This combination of rock, mud and sand could be a good spot for **coastal botanising**.

DISTRIBUTION

As we saw in the previous section, many plants are very discriminating about where they will grow - there are habitats they prefer and habitats they avoid. Differing habitats come about because of variations in underlying rock, rainfall, sunshine, altitude and so on; they are therefore distributed in certain patterns around the country. We have already looked at a rainfall map and a temperature map of the British Isles under 'moisture' (see page 61). If we combine this with maps of altitude and basic (alkaline) rocks, and note that built-up areas will usually support fewer wild plants, we begin to see the reasons for the wide variation in local flora throughout the country.

Geography

There is little to prevent the special plants of basic grassland from growing in Scotland - it's just that Scotland is rather short on basic grassland. However, in the few pockets where it exists - such as Ben Lawers - those special plants may indeed turn up, unless limited by other factors such as temperature or altitude. Similarly, the plants characteristic of north country mountains might well grow in the southeast of England - if it possessed any mountains.

Alpine gentian (blue) is one of the specialities of Ben Lawers, a mountain that is a mecca for many botanists, being one of the few limestone areas in highland Scotland.

Another factor in this equation is pollution. Some plants are much more sensitive to pollution than others. These delicate souls may make their home on mountains not so much because they are fond of heights or prefer the cooler climes, but because it is the best place to escape the effects of pollution from built-up and busy areas.

Frost is also a variable in a small island group such as Britain. Did your geography teacher impress upon you Britain's 'warm, wet, westerly winds in winter'? Plants which cannot tolerate frost or prolonged snow-lie will thrive in western coastal areas where hard frosts are few and far between.

*Areas of **high ground** in the British Isles.*

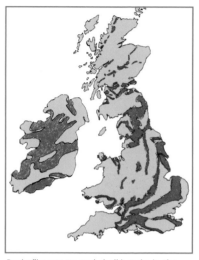

Basic (limestone and chalk) rocks in the British Isles.

LOCAL FLOWERS

In 2002, the conservation charity Plantlife asked people to vote for a wild flower to represent their county. Tens of thousands of votes were received and each county of the British Isles was given its own floral emblem. Interestingly, some are clearly 'botanists' choices': rare and obscure plants that local botanists are proud to have in their county, such as Fife's coralroot orchid and Westmorland's alpine forget-me-not. Others, however, are familiar (and clearly much-loved) wild flowers which are common everywhere - foxglove, for example, was the choice of Leicestershire, Argyll and Monmouthshire. Several counties understandably chose a plant named after the county or a place within it, such as Radnor lily, Shetland mouse-ear, Cheddar pink (Somerset), Cornish heath, Scottish primrose (Caithness) and Chiltern gentian (Buckinghamshire). The full list can be found at www.plantlife.org.uk (click on 'discovering wild plants').

It is a fascinating exercise to study the distribution map of a particular plant, comparing it with various geographical maps, and try to work out what features - latitude, rainfall, aspect and so on - determine where that plant will and won't grow. It's not an exact science, though. Some plants never make it to a place that would suit them down to the ground (as it were); others inexplicably decline to settle in what looks like the ideal spot. (Orchid-growing in captivity was hampered for a long time because it was not understood that orchids need certain fungi in the soil around their roots in order to flourish.) Teasing out the factors that help a plant to grow in a certain place is one of the deeper delights of field botany.

We have already encountered the Lundy cabbage (page 12) and on page 80 you will find the story of the Oxford ragwort. The following list is of flowering plants which have common names denoting the locality in which they were first discovered or which is especially famed for them. Can you complete any of these names?

Kerry _ _ _ _   Deptford _ _ _ _   Cambridge _ _ _ _   _ _ _ _ _ _ _

Teesdale _ _ _ _ _ _   Portland _ _ _ _ _ _   Nottingham _ _ _ _ _ _ _ _

Tenby _ _ _ _ _ _ _ _   Plymouth _ _ _ _ _ _ _ or _ _ _ _

Answers on page 88

*Westmorland's county flower, **alpine forget-me-not**, is a rare plant of limestone grassland in mountains such as the northern Pennines. It is a brighter blue than its lowland relatives.*

*The county flower chosen by Somerset is the **Cheddar pink**. The limestone rocks of Cheddar gorge are its only home in Britain. (Are 'pinks' so called because they are often coloured pink? Or because the margins of their petals are often 'pinked' i.e. notched or scalloped? No-one is quite sure.)*

Mapping

When we take into account all the various habitat features plus geographical limitations, add some serendipity and subtract some bad luck, we find out where plants actually do grow - their distribution.

In some fieldguides, you will see little maps down the margins showing the parts of the British Isles in which you may hope to find the plant in question. These are often very helpful in deciding whether you have a 'match' with the species described in the book. Let's say you are looking at what seems to be a bedstraw (a *Galium* species) with a cluster of white flowers and whorls of leaves round the stem. Judging by the illustrations and descriptions, you feel it could be just about any one of the dozen species in the book. Taking a glance at the maps, however, you discover that six of them have a very limited distribution, whereas the others are found throughout the country. Remembering the naturalists' dictum that 'common things are common' the likelihood is that you can halve the number of possible answers and so make your task a great deal easier.

Or suppose you have found a tall, not very prickly thistle with a vivid purple flower. You may decide it's a choice between melancholy thistle (*Cirsium*

heterophyllum) and meadow thistle (*Cirsium dissectum*). But look at the maps and your problem is instantly solved: the distributions of melancholy and meadow thistles barely overlap at all - if you're in the north, it's melancholy, if in the south it's meadow thistle and that's more or less it. (In a very few places, it could conceivably be either.) Incidentally the distribution here also gives you a clue as to why the two are so alike; it is reasonable to speculate that at one time they were a single species, evolving in slightly different ways until they became separate species.

*This **melancholy thistle** is very similar to its southern relative. The plant was once used as a treatment for melancholia i.e. depression - and a patch of its tall stems by a roadside or riverbank is certainly a cheering sight.*

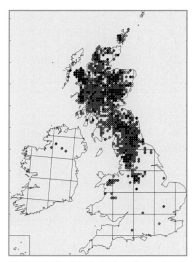

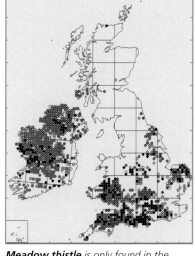

Melancholy thistle *is virtually confined to the northern half of the country.*

Meadow thistle *is only found in the southern half and Ireland.*

These two maps are often called 'dot maps.' Distribution maps may also be presented in a more simplified form as shaded or coloured areas showing the range of the plant in question, perhaps with two or more colours denoting the plant's abundance within its range. Distribution maps in general handbooks are likely to be based on those in the 'Atlas 2000', as it is known. The Atlas was compiled with the help of many field botanists, both amateur and professional, recording all the plants they could find in a square measuring 10 km by 10 km. Dot maps were drawn up in which each dot represents the presence of the species in that square.

How many different species of plants do you suppose are to be found in the average 10 km square? 100? 200? In fact, the majority of squares each contain more than 500 species! In a square in a 'species-poor' area

*You may be surprised at how **many species** you can find in quite a small area: in this picture there are forget-me-nots, globe flowers (a member of the Buttercup family) and cowslips, along with several others.*

an expert botanist (perhaps making several visits over the season) might still expect to find 200 or so species. While 'number-crunching' is not the name of the game, you may still be agreeably surprised at how the number of species mounts up in even quite an unambitious excursion of your own.

Commonest plants

Another question that sometimes fascinates, but is very difficult to answer, is 'Which is the commonest British species?' Before attempting to answer it, we should look at some of the terms botanists use to indicate how common a species is. The usual line-up is as follows:

abundant	you are almost bound to find it in suitable habitats
common	very likely to be found in most suitable places
frequent	quite likely to be found in some places but not in others
occasional	you might need to search hard in several areas before you find it
rare	unlikely to be found unless you know exactly when and where to look - and you'll need a bit of luck into the bargain.

These ratings, though, need to be taken with a few caveats. In the first place, all the above categories assume that you are looking in the right sort of place. However abundant daisies may be throughout these islands, you're still not going to find them in ponds. Secondly, the categories are most useful in local floras. For example, while bog asphodel might be rated as 'abundant' in a flora of northern Scotland, it may be rated as 'rare' in a flora of East Anglia or the Midlands. In addition, some species have a habit of growing in 'stands' containing hundreds of one species all in one place. Others prefer their own company - one grows here, one there, and one somewhere else entirely. Both types might amount to the same number of plants in a given area such as a 10 km square, but because of the bunching effect, you may have different kinds of problems in trying to spot them.

*If you see a boggy heath liberally dotted with bright orange-yellow flowers, you are fairly certain to be looking at **bog asphodel**. Once the flowers are over, the whole plant appears as a deep orange spike, which often persists for many months.*

To return to the question 'Which is the commonest British species?' Is it the one that has the largest number of individual plants? Or the one that is found in the greatest variety of habitats? Or the one that is most widespread throughout the country? The third question looks easy enough to answer by studying distribution maps, but as we have seen, simply being recorded in a 10 km square doesn't necessarily imply that there are lots of individual specimens. If a plant is recorded as being present in a hundred squares, there might be just a single plant in each square - a total of a hundred plants. On the other hand, another species might be recorded in just one square, but be represented there by hundreds or even thousands of plants. Which is the commoner species?

In 2006 the Countryside Survey attempted to answer the 'commonest plant?' question by sampling. Studying more than eighteen thousand random plots right across the UK, the survey first looked at which forbs (herbs, not counting grasses etc.) were found most frequently. In the second place, they looked at which forbs covered the largest areas of ground in those plots. Interestingly, both methods produced very similar results. Here are the two lists of their findings:

MOST FREQUENT

1	Stinging nettle	Urtica dioica
2	Creeping buttercup	Ranunculus repens
3	White clover	Trifolium repens
4	Cleavers	Galium aparine
5	Dandelion	Taraxacum agg (i.e. various species & subspecies)
6	Creeping thistle	Cirsium arvense
7	Mouse-ear	Cerastium fontanum
8	Cow parsley	Anthriscus sylvestris
9	Heath bedstraw	Galium saxatile
10	Meadow buttercup	Ranunculus acris

LARGEST AREA

1	Stinging nettle	Urtica dioica
2	Creeping buttercup	Ranunculus repens
3	Cleavers	Galium aparine
4	Creeping thistle	Cirsium arvense
5	Cow parsley	Anthriscus sylvestris
6	Hogweed	Heracleum sphondylium
7	Meadowsweet	Filipendula ulmaria
8	Dandelion	Taraxacum agg
9	Tormentil	Potentilla erecta
10	Ground ivy	Glechoma hederacea

Clover and buttercups, *two of the commonest forbs in Britain.*

Diverse distributions

As we see from the table, the most common plants are found nationwide. However, the distribution of species around the country is affected by many factors. One species may reach its northern limit in Britain so it will disappear from the map part of the way up. For a different species, there may be an east-west divide, due to frost-tolerance or rainfall requirements.

Spignel, *a feathery-leaved umbellifer, is a rare plant of hill pastures.*

A third may be absent from land over two thousand feet. Another may be scattered about wherever basic soils are to be found. Where the distribution dots appear only round the edges of the map, we're clearly looking at a species that clings to coastal habitats. Built-up areas will be dot-free for plants whose motto is 'do not disturb.' So the map of each individual species will be unique, reflecting all the factors that affect its own distribution.

A recent survey found that lists of the top twenty most successful species in the north and the south of Britain overlapped very little, even though all the species were common throughout the country. For example, meadow buttercup was high on the northern list, but not in the south's top twenty at all, whereas with ragwort it was the other way round. Of forbs, only daisies, white clover and ribwort plantain appeared in both lists.

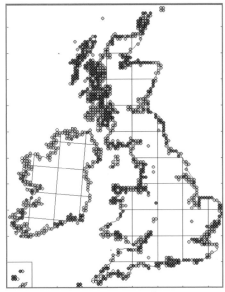

*Map of a coastal species: **sea milkwort**.*

***Salt marshes** and **shingle** are sometimes densely covered with the tiny pink flowers of **sea milkwort**. What appear to be the petals are actually the pink sepals. The distribution map shows it to be almost entirely a coastal plant.*

RAGWORT BY RAIL

Towards the end of the seventeenth century, a certain species of ragwort, not native to Britain, was brought from its home on the volcanic ash of Mount Etna in Italy to be planted in the Oxford Botanic Gardens. By the end of the following century the plant, now known as Oxford ragwort (*Senecio squalidus*), was found to have escaped from the Botanic Gardens and to be sunning itself on the the old stone walls of various Oxford colleges. Then the railways were built.

The seeds of Oxford ragwort floated down from the stone walls of the buildings on to the clinker beds of the Great Western Railway - and found their ideal home. By the close of the nineteenth century the new plant had been noted in Warwickshire and Devon; by the time of the first world war it had been recorded in Wales. Eventually it spread all the way to Scotland. Now, almost everywhere you go on a railway journey you can see Oxford ragwort's bright yellow flowers (very like our native common ragwort, but with a distinctive 'jizz' that you will soon master if you look for it) from your carriage window. Even where Dr Beeching's axe descended in the 1960s, Oxford ragwort may still be seen along former railway routes. Without understanding the railway connection, the distribution of Oxford ragwort would be a puzzle indeed.

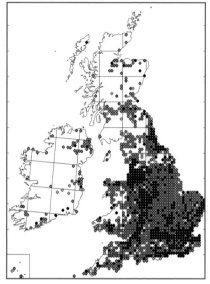

Distribution of **Oxford ragwort**, an introduced plant that has spread from Oxford to the far reaches of the British Isles.

Oxford ragwort first escaped from the Oxford Botanic Garden in 1794 and has since colonised a large part of Britain, especially near railways and on waste ground. It begins to flower in April, two months earlier than the native ragwort.

PLACES TO BOTANISE

Putting together the knowledge we have gained about habitats and distribution we can now consider the kinds of places where botanising can be fruitful and fun, and what kinds of plants we may expect to find in them.

Towns and cities

Although one can botanise wherever there's a niche for a plant to survive in, naturally the wilder places tend to support the wilder plants. Nevertheless, in a town street you may find quite a few plants taking a walk on the wild side. These tend to be one of two kinds. The first kind are the 'weeds' that grow just as happily in the town as in the countryside - daisies and dandelions, groundsel, chickweed, plantains and so on. It's well worth getting your eye in for these common plants, so that you can recognise their 'jizz' wherever you find them. (Though be careful not to make assumptions - one small difference might mean you are looking at a separate species.) In some cases, knowing one familiar member of a group will be a great help when you meet a less common one. There are many yellow composites, for example, that look awfully like dandelions; but they don't look *exactly* like them, so if you have a good acquaintance with dandelions you will be immediately alerted by something that looks just that little bit different.

*You know these are **dandelions**, but <u>how</u> do you know? The pappus (clock) is white - some other look-alikes have a brownish pappus. There is only one flower per stem - others have a branched stem with several flowers. Very few look-alikes have the dandelion's large, brownish, down-turned outer ring of 'sepals' (called 'phyllaries' in the composites).*

The second kind of plant most likely to be found in towns is the alien. There is no shame in being an alien, it's just that identifying them is often much harder, because they may not appear in your fieldguide unless they are fairly widespread. I remember the first time I found garden lobelias growing in pavement cracks: it took me ages to work out what they were, until I cottoned on to the connection between these tiny multicoloured flowers and the very same ones growing in hanging baskets above my head!

Parks and gardens

Your own - or someone else's - garden is another fruitful area, especially if the resident gardener is not too much of a stickler for weed-removal. The same applies to urban parks and open spaces, and also to cemeteries and churchyards. The question you have to address here is whether your specimen was deliberately planted (or is the offspring of something planted) as this isn't always immediately obvious. Generally speaking, the more tidy and regimented the garden or park appears, the more likely it is that the plant in question is there on purpose.

Waste ground

A patch of waste ground, such as a building site, rubbish dump, quarry or parking area, may throw up quite a mix of interesting plants. (N.B. In all such places, safety must take priority over botany; see pages 134 to 136 for how to botanise safely.) Some of these plants will be annuals whose seeds may have remained in the soil (the seedbank) for years, just waiting their chance to flourish when the competition from established plants is reduced. Others could be garden throw-outs or escapes, some may have come from seed deposited in bird droppings or have been brought in with soil from elsewhere. Rare orchids have occasionally been found on slag heaps, where the discarded mining products are particularly suited to their growth.

Knapweed, tansy, yarrow, broom and chicory are some of the plants that have colonised this rich piece of **waste ground.**

HIGHWAY HERBAGE

Don't stop to check, but motorway verges provide a refuge for a number of plants that are now quite rare elsewhere. The M40 in Buckinghamshire, for example, is home to some green-winged orchids and the M50 sports genuinely wild daffodils, while stinking hellebore graces the M90 just outside Perth.

In total, the verges of motorways and trunk roads in Britain amount to some 27,000 hectares - about the size of the Isle of Wight. Although some native wild flowers have been deliberately planted, others simply take advantage of the lack of disturbance, including pyramidal, lady and bee orchids. Other uncommon roadside plants are coralroot (a rare bittercress) in West Sussex, Spanish catchfly in Cambridgeshire and bastard toadflax (a member of the Sandalwood family) in Lincolnshire.

A fascinating feature is the spread of coastal plants which thrive on the salt used on icy roads in winter. Danish scurvygrass can be seen alongside many major roads, while sea-spurrey and buckshorn plantain are increasingly common there. Considering the butterflies and other insects that visit the plants, the many small rodents that scurry among them, and the kestrels that hunt the rodents, it is no wonder that highway verges have been described as 'Britain's least-known nature reserve'.

Danish scurvygrass (left), originally a coastal plant, now borders the verges and central reservations of many main roads which are salted in winter, flowering from January onwards. **English scurvygrass** (below) doesn't begin flowering until April, and is confined to estuaries and muddy seashores.

Water features

Some plants only thrive in wet places, while others use moving water as a means of transport from one place to another. So any kind of water feature - rivers and canals, lakes, ponds, ditches and drains - is likely to be productive from a botanical point of view. The seashore is somewhat different, as plants that live within spitting distance of the sea need to be tolerant of salt. Many seashore plants are not found anywhere else, though some plants such as scurvygrass can increasingly be seen along the edges of trunk roads which are salted in winter but otherwise little disturbed.

Countryside

The 'real' countryside is obviously the mecca for most people going botanising. The range of habitats in the British Isles is vast and the floral variety likewise. We are especially lucky to have such a chequer-board of different kinds of countryside all within relatively easy reach. It can hardly be so much fun for a botanist living on the edge of the Sahara or in the middle of a vast monocultural conifer plantation in Canada, for example! Whether you're going on a family picnic or a long-distance trek over the hills, you're bound to find a selection of interesting plants to study.

*Here **thrift** has taken advantage of the soil formed by other plants in the midst of a shingle beach.*

Hotspots

As you become accustomed to searching your surroundings for interesting plants, you will notice that, although there may be large areas that are rather 'samey', some smaller pockets can be quite different from the rest. Such **microhabitats** may have a richer flora due to conditions that favour plants other than the dominant ones all around.

Edges of anything may be richer in plants than centres. For example, the edge of a wood or field, the side of a path, the margin of a water feature and so on, may have the best of both worlds and support plants from both types of habitat.

Edges *are often good botanising spots; here the edge of a small stream is home to a number of different forbs, grasses and ferns.*

Damp hollows and flushes (where surface water flows gently rather than sinking into the ground) often harbour special plants not to be found in the drier areas in between.

At the other end of the scale, small **dry** areas, such as mounds or ridges might have a different set of plants from the wet bogs and fens round about.

South-facing slopes, which receive sunshine at a shallower angle than north-facing ones and thus more of it, tend to be richer.

Inaccessible ledges and steep cliffs, which grazing animals cannot reach, may harbour some of the rarest plants of all - but unless you are into abseiling, you will not be able to reach them either! This is where a good pair of binoculars comes in very handy.

Surveying the scene

In general, where conditions change, the flora will tend to change as well, so it helps to take an overall look at the area and make a mental note of which parts look most promising. Survey the terrain as a whole, and ask yourself what the prevailing conditions are in any particular part of it - damp or dry, sunny or shady, high or low, settled or disturbed.

*The differently coloured patches in this scene are the clue to different **microhabitats** and thus to differing suites of plants. In this particular case, varying degrees of water-logging are probably responsible for the change in vegetation from one part to the next.*

Suppose, for example, you are standing on a path beside a large meadow where cattle are grazing; behind a fence on the far side there is a wood. Look first at the colours, especially the shades of green. Where the green is deepest with a bluer tinge, will be the dampest and richest areas; a patch of buttercups is a dead giveaway for a damp hollow, as is the creamy-white of meadowsweet or a stand of tall rushes. If it is very marshy, you might see the blazing gold of marsh marigolds, or perhaps the bright blue of water forget-me-nots. In more acid conditions, sedges are more likely, perhaps accompanied by purple-pink louseworts or yellow bog asphodel. Nearest the path or elsewhere on thin soil - such as over rocky ground - the grass will be paler and more yellowish; here there may be plantains, yarrow, daisies, shepherd's purse and so on. Beyond the fence, where the cattle cannot stray, the grass will be taller and paler, but under the trees grass may give way to bluebells (if you're lucky) or maybe dog's mercury (green-flowered), wood anemone (white) or ground ivy (mauve).

So even from a distance you can pick out different habitat areas which are worth going to take a closer look at. By the reverse token, the appearance of marsh-loving plants warns you to watch your step if you're not wearing your wellies!

BOTANIST AS DETECTIVE

Wetness underfoot is not the only thing that botanists may have the edge on in detective work. The presence of nettles, for example, (and also cleavers and elderberry) tells you that phosphates are in the soil and phosphates are a clue to human and animal activities. Where these plants are rife, they often indicate a long-abandoned midden (refuse heap) perhaps associated with the ruins of buildings - or occasionally, in the wilder places, with a farmer's covert burial of a dead sheep! Nettles may also be found at the entrances to burrows, setts, etc. where animal droppings have accumulated.

Former woodland may also leave its mark in the flora: in some years you may see a carpet of bluebells in an open pasture, which tells you that at one time this was almost certainly an ancient wood. Wood anemone and wood sorrel on ground that is now treeless tell the same story. On the other hand, an area of young birch trees suggests that the land here has been left to its own devices, possibly after burning, since they are usually the first trees to colonise neglected spots. Ancient grassland which has not been ploughed for hundreds of years can be the botanist's seventh heaven, containing many rare and special plants that only survive where the ground has never been disturbed.

Birches are rarely deliberately sown - they don't have to be. Where other plants have been destroyed - by grazing, felling, fire etc. - and no positive management has taken place, birches are one of the most likely trees to become established.

*In the British Isles, the **Kerry lily** is only found in Co. Kerry in the far southwest of Ireland, although it also crops up on some western European seaboards.*

*The **Deptford pink** is no longer to be found in Deptford, and is one of our plants which is sadly decreasing. However, it can still be seen in a few dry grassy places in the south.*

NAME THAT PLANT

Putting a name to a plant satisfies our instinctive desire to identify what we see. It is also the indispensable first step in any botanical activity. In times past, naming was imperative for identifying plants to be eaten or used for medicinal, ritual and other purposes. Even today, members of some tribal societies can name hundreds of the plants required for their daily lives. Our reasons are usually rather different - labelling photographs and drawings, for example, not pulling up the wrong things on a conservation project, or just the sheer pleasure of knowing which plant is which. But for whatever reason, plants need to be named.

One of the chief aims of this book is to help you go about the business of identification in an informed and systematic way. In this chapter we come to the heart of the matter: how to proceed from observations to names.

Lacking the traditional knowledge of plants possessed by our distant forbears, the essential tool for us is a fieldguide: a handbook with plant descriptions, illustrations, keys and tables to guide us towards correct identifications. Before discussing fieldguides, though, we are going to look at how plants are classified, since the more authoritative fieldguides are arranged more or less in order of scientific classification.

HOW PLANTS ARE CLASSIFIED

The order of plants in a good fieldguide is generally the order in which plants are understood to have evolved, with the oldest (most 'primitive') first, through to the most recently evolved at the end. However, ideas on plant classification are never completely static, and DNA data is increasingly being used to supplant visible features for deciding where a plant should be placed in the scheme of things. (It is rumoured that the field botanist's lens will one day be replaced by a hand-held DNA analyser. But I rather hope not.) Scientific names are sometimes changed to reflect new data and fresh theories of classification. And although there is supposed to be a standardised set of English names to match, not every writer defers to it. The present book, for example, does not capitalise the English names of plant species, only those of families, on the grounds that such formality is more appropriately confined to scientific names. So you may occasionally find different names used for the same plant - a minor source of confusion to beginners which can usually be resolved by consulting several accounts. But in general, it is well worth gaining familiarity with both the vernacular (English) names and the scientific (Latin) ones.

We have already seen that the Plant Kingdom is divided into flowering and non-flowering plants, and that the flowering plants are effectively split again into monocots and dicots. Apart from some divisions that don't much concern anyone except professional botanists, the next level down is the family. Families have already entered our discussions and include such groups as Roses, Crucifers, Cranesbills, Umbellifers and so on. Within each family will be one or more **genus** (plural: genera) and within the genus one or more **species** (which is both singular and plural).

*Not an easy plant to identify! By narrowing down the possibilities, this plant was first classed as a composite (from the flower design), then as a ragwort (from the structure of the individual florets), but not a native ragwort. It was finally tracked down from its unusual leaves as a rare alien called **Chinese ragwort**.*

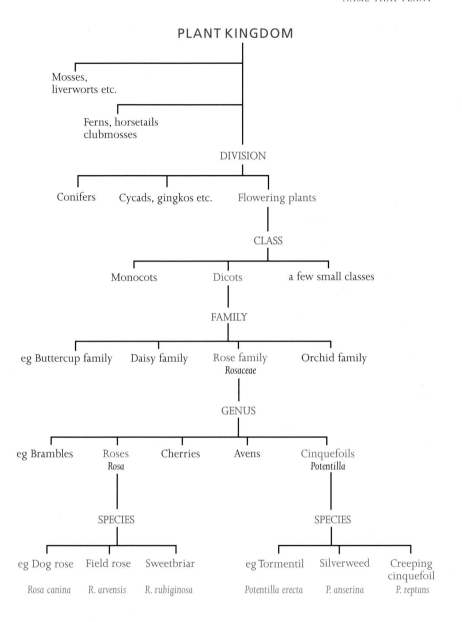

This chart highlights two genera, the roses (*Rosa*) and the cinquefoils (*Potentilla*), both members of the Rose family, giving examples of three species within each genus.

The species level is what we are usually seeking in an identification, though there are also subspecies, varieties and hybrids between species which will no doubt start to intrigue you when the botany-bug really bites.

A few names in Latin have been used already in this book (e.g. *Spartina anglica* on page 56 and *Senecio squalidus* on page 80), and you will notice from the table that a species always has a scientific name in two parts e.g. *Potentilla anserina* (silverweed), *Rosa canina* (dog rose). The first is the name of the genus, otherwise called the **generic name**, and it is always written with a capital letter (except in ignorant newspaper reports). The second, without a capital letter, is the name of the species, or **specific name**.

All plants of the same **species** have the same flowers, leaves, stem etc. However, features such as precise flower colour or overall plant height may vary within a species, according to growing conditions (as gardeners will appreciate who have aspired to turn a blue hydrangea pink).

All species within the same **genus** will have many similarities, especially in flower design, but also some differences. For example, tormentil is also a member of the *Potentilla* genus to which silverweed belongs.

Silverweed *Potentilla anserina* (above) has five petals and its leaves are silvery on the underside. **Tormentil** *Potentilla erecta* (right) has four petals (unusual in the Rose family) and the leaves are green on both sides.

Tormentil is called *P. erecta* (if you have just mentioned the genus in question, it is OK simply to put the P again without writing out the whole word *Potentilla*). Like silverweed, tormentil is yellow with very similar flowers and leaves. However, tormentil only has four petals and its leaves are green above and below, whereas silverweed has five petals and the leaves are silvery underneath (hence the name).

All genera within the same **family** will have reproductive parts that are pretty much alike, but the flowers may be different colours in various types of flowerhead, the leaves differently shaped or arranged and so on. For example, compare cinquefoils such as silverweed and tormentil with roses, brambles and strawberries: however different they may appear at first glance, all these genera in fact belong to the Rose family. Typical members of the Rose family have five petals, numerous stamens, alternate leaves, and **stipules** (small leaf-like structures where the leaf-stalk joins the stem).

*Consider how much **roses** have in common with silverweed (previous page) - saucer-shaped, five-petalled flowers with numerous stamens, alternate leaves and stipules (the last is hard to see in these pictures though).*

WHY LATIN?

Although there has been a recent resurgence of interest in Latin, few younger people have what used to be called 'the benefit of a classical education'. The thought of having to learn scientific names in a dead language might be a bit off-putting, so why bother?

While most birdwatchers and butterfly-fanciers manage without too much Latin, botanists have many more species to contend with, some of which are very similar. Vernacular names for some species are legion and often vary from one locality to another. Cow parsley, for example, may be called Queen Anne's lace, devil's parsley, keck, wild chervil and even hemlock. To avoid confusion, every serious botanist the world over will know it also as *Anthriscus sylvestris*. This ensures that we are all talking about the same plant, and not the various other plants also known colloquially as chervil, hemlock etc. This is not to say that botanists use scientific names exclusively - you might get some funny looks if you said 'Oh look, it's a *Bellis perennis*!' Everyone says 'daisy' unless they're making an official record.

Cow parsley *has so many local names that the scientific name Anthriscus sylvestris is essential to pin down which plant you are talking about. Sylvestris means 'of the woods', which in this case are mainly shady hedgebanks.*

One of the useful results of knowing at least some scientific names is that they often give you a clue as to what feature is particularly characteristic of that plant. For example, look at the names of some violets:

Viola odorata	sweet violet	*odorata* means sweet-smelling
Viola hirta	hairy violet	*hirta* means hairy
Viola lactea	pale dog violet	*lactea* means milky
Viola tricolor	wild pansy	*tricolor* means three-coloured

If you think of English words like 'odour', 'hirsute' and 'lactation' the Latin species name tells you what to expect; in the case of 'tricolor', the three colours of the wild pansy are yellow and purple with an orange tinge in the centre. (Note: although scientific names are formulated as if they were in Latin, their roots are sometimes Greek or other languages.)

More importantly, even though two different words, 'violet' and 'pansy', are used in English, the scientific name indicates that they all belong to the same genus, so you know they are going to have many features in common. By contrast, the plant known in English as 'water violet' belongs to the genus *Hottonia*, a member of the Primrose family, and the butterworts are often known as 'bog violets' but are actually *Pinguicula* species, from the Bladderwort family; neither of these 'violets' come from the Violet family.

Marsh violets *Viola palustris (above) are true members of the Violet family, whereas* **common butterwort** *Pinguicula vulgaris, also known as bog violet, belongs to the Bladderwort family. From the front, the flowers do look a bit similar, but a sideways view shows that the butterwort petals are joined and tapered into a spur at the back.*

FIELDGUIDES AND HOW TO USE THEM

Most of the books you will find on the botany shelves of your local library or bookshop will be fieldguides of one kind or another. But how to choose the one that will be most useful to you? Some cover the whole of the British Isles, or even the whole of Europe, while some are limited to a particular area (Scotland, say) or a particular habitat (the seashore, for instance). As a companion to the present book, the handiest would be one restricted to the British Isles, and that mentions virtually every plant you may find, rather than merely a selection - otherwise it could be just your luck to have found a plant that is not in the guide.

In your bookshop or bookseller's website you may find a bewildering array of fieldguides and floras to choose from. (The word **'flora'** can be used to mean 'a publication listing all the plants of an area' or simply 'the flowering plants of an area'.) A local flora (first sense) might be simply a checklist: a record of all the plants to be found, but without descriptions of them. On the other hand, a local flora might list, describe and illustrate, but only the notable or special plants of the area. Then again, a handbook covering the whole of the British Isles may only deal with common plants, those the author reckons you are most likely to come across. So your best bet - especially if you're only buying one book - is to try for a comprehensive manual covering all plants and all areas, with pictures, descriptions and - with any luck - maps too.

Fieldguides may be arranged by habitat, by colour, by season or some other criterion, in the hope that this will make it easier for beginners to find their way about. There are obvious disadvantages to all these partial expositions. It is earnestly hoped that by the time you have absorbed all the information in the present book, you will feel ready to use a more 'professional' fieldguide:

Playing 'snap' with a book and a plant.

one that describes in scientific order every native species, whether common or rare, and possibly the commoner subspecies, hybrids and aliens as well. But don't throw away any books about plants you already possess; it is often useful to compare descriptions and illustrations from several books, to be absolutely certain of an identification.

Recommended books

The authority for most field botanists is Clive Stace's **New Flora of the British Isles** (first published in 1991, 3rd edition 2010) but this has one big drawback for those just starting out: it has very few pictures (Alice in Wonderland wouldn't have liked it). A serious botanist cannot manage without 'Stace', but an illustrated book is clearly necessary as well, since botany is so much a visual occupation.

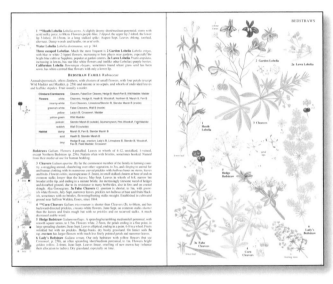

Pages from **Wild Flowers of Britain & Ireland**, *with descriptions, illustrations, maps and tables to aid identification.*

One of the better illustrated books is **Wild Flowers of Britain & Ireland** with paintings by Marjorie Blamey and text by Richard and Alastair Fitter, published by A & C Black in 2003. This has good pictures, including details of flowers and leaves, plus distribution maps and descriptions which help to distinguish possible look-alikes. A bonus is that trees, shrubs, grasses and sedges are also covered and there is a well-illustrated glossary. Francis Rose's **The Wild Flower Key** (edition of 2006) is a very authoritative handbook. Though perhaps a little less easy for the beginner to follow, it does reduce the temptation to play 'snap', as it concentrates on showing the critical differences between related species; it also has very useful keys to groups of species, one of which we will study later in this chapter. Other fieldguides come and go, but many dedicated amateur botanists tend to keep Francis Rose's text and Marjorie Blamey's paintings as their trusted companions.

There are a number of fieldguides on the market which employ photographs rather than paintings. It is quite useful to have one of these as nothing captures the 'jizz' of a plant quite as well as a photo, and they generally give a good idea of how the plant appears in its habitat which can be very helpful. However, they have their limitations as far as identification is concerned since it is difficult to demonstrate every diagnostic feature in a photo. So for meticulous accuracy a more detailed guide will also be needed.

Many families with a bent towards natural history will have a copy of 'Keble Martin' (*The Concise British Flora in Colour*). Published back in 1965 and long out of print (though often cropping up in secondhand bookshops), this is still a valuable reference book to be going on with. The drawings are first class (but not so the printed colours) although the descriptions of plants are extremely brief. One rather endearing feature of this book is that although it has both an English and a scientific (Latin) index at the back, the English names don't lead you to a page number, only to the scientific names; that way, you learn the scientific names without tears.

Getting the best from a fieldguide

Countless hours have been whiled away by novice botanists with a flower in one hand and a book in the other, vainly attempting to find a match between the two by perusing every page in the book. Ask yourself whether you would approach any other search in such a chaotic manner - such as looking for a town by studying an atlas of the whole world, inch by inch, until you find the one you want, rather than by establishing first what country it is in and so on down. (Nowadays, of course, Google is the answer to many searches, but until you can scan in your living plant and use the OPR (Optical Plant Recognition) software provided, Google's help is limited to its 'image' facility.)

It's a yellow composite, but doesn't look much like a dandelion - more like a cross between ragwort, goldenrod and pineappleweed, you say? So try looking on pages where these three are to be found and you will soon discover that this is **tansy**.

In the long run, it is going to be quicker to understand how the plant world is organised so that you can eliminate the no-go areas, progressively homing in on a family, then a genus and finally a species. Get acquainted with your fieldguide by looking through it at leisure - not just when you are in a hurry to identify a particular plant - and establish in your mind whereabouts within it various kinds of plants are to be found. If your specimen looks rather like one you are already familiar with - not merely in colour, but in flower design, number of petals and so on - then you already have a clue about where you might find it.

Here is a list of the characters we have examined in this book:

- plant type and growth habit
- hairiness
- flower colour, size and arrangement
- fruit
- flower design
- habitat
- design and arrangement of leaves
- distribution

Use all of them as far as you are able, not just the one that is most striking to your eye. When you think you are getting warm, begin to study the illustrations and descriptions in more detail. You may find that your fieldguide divides the larger families into smaller, more easily-managed groups. For example, the Composites might be subdivided into daisy-type, thistle-type and dandelion-type. If you are able to class your specimen as one or other of these subgroups, clearly the task of identification will be much more direct.

Three main sections in the Composite (Asteraceae) family: daisies, thistles and dandelions.

Most good fieldguides will have a method - such as **bold** or *italic* typeface - of alerting you to characters that distinguish similar species. For example, if you see 'flowers *yellow*' in one species description, where that of the next species says 'flowers *white*', you will know that colour difference is crucial in distinguishing these two species. Or the descriptions might contrast 'found in *wet* places' with 'found in *dry* places' or 'leaves *opposite*' with 'leaves *alternate*' and so on. Some books may have pointers in the illustrations to indicate which are the critical distinguishing features, or include enlarged drawings to pick out important details. Check here whether the main illustrations are life size, or whether they have merely been designed to fit the page.

Using keys

Now a word about keys. Many fieldguides provide keys to the complete flora, to the members of a family, or to a difficult group. The 'easy' handbooks may key by colour, habitat, season or size, and these keys can be helpful to the complete beginner in pointing you in the right direction (though occasionally in an utterly wrong direction). Better still are keys using number of petals and/or type of flowerhead, as these approach more closely the scientific classification. Another easy-to-follow device is the table; here is an example from Blamey & Fitter, to elucidate the Cranesbills.

Petals	deeply-notched:	Hedgerow, Dovesfoot, Small-flowered, Cut-leaved
	shallowly-notched:	Purple, Wood, Bloody, French, Pencilled, Round-leaved, Long-stalked
	not notched:	Meadow, Wood, Herb Robert, Little Robin, Shining, Round-leaved, Long-stalked

*The **shallowly-notched** **petals** limit the possibilities for this cranesbill, but other data is needed as well; in this case the leaves suggest **wood cranesbill**.*

The fact that some species, e.g. wood cranesbill, appear in two places indicates that their petals are sometimes shallowly-notched but sometimes not at all - an example of variation within a species.

The next example is of a branching key (though not an exhaustive one) to the commoner poppies. The principle is that at each stage (numbered from 1 upwards) you choose between two mutually exclusive options. The one you choose will either tell you what plant it is, or direct you to another number. At the number you are sent to, you will find two more options, and so on until you get the final answer. Or not, as sometimes happens. In that case, you go back to your specimen, study it even more closely, and start all over again, checking that you do really understand the terms used in the key and aren't just guessing.

1a	Petals red	(go to) 5
b	Petals not red	2
2a	Petals yellow	4
b	Petals not yellow	3
3a	Petals lilac	Opium Poppy
b	Petals not lilac	other garden escape
4a	Sprawling on coastal shingle; leaves silvery, seedpods long & curved	Yellow Horned-poppy
b	Stoney places, or near gardens; leaves green, seedpods egg-shaped	Welsh Poppy
5a	Smaller crimson flowers, seedpod covered in bristles (S & Midlands only)	Rough Poppy
b	Larger scarlet flowers, no bristles on seedpods	6
6a	Flowers slightly pinkish, probably without black centre, seedpods long & thin, ridged	Long-headed Poppy
b	Flowers true scarlet, probably black-centred, seedpods round	Common Poppy

On page 112 you will find a worked example using a genuinely exhaustive branching key. Meanwhile, next time you come across a poppy, run through the key above and see if you can put a definite name to it.

*It's yellow and it's on coastal shingle - is it a yellow horned-poppy? No, because the leaves are green and the seedpods egg-shaped. It's a **Welsh poppy,** but outside Wales is likely to be a garden escape, often to be seen in places such as this stony Scottish beach.*

STRATEGIES FOR IDENTIFICATION

As we saw at the beginning of this chapter, putting a name to a plant you have found is both a natural desire and an indispensable part of any botanical activity. So here you are with an unnamed plant in front of you and a fieldguide with the power to supply you with a name. How can you put that power to use?

*To identify this plant as **common vetch** requires attention not just to the individual flowers, but also to their arrangement and to the leaves and tendrils.*

If you have followed the suggestions offered so far, you will be able to describe your plant in the following terms:

flower:	colour
	design
	number of petals
	type of flowerhead
leaves:	simple or compound
	shape, margins, etc.
	relation to stem
plant:	hairiness
	habit
	scent, if any
	fruit, if available
situation:	habitat
	location
	flowering season

The details of flower and leaf should be clear in the illustrations in your fieldguide, and most or all of the plant and situation characters will be found in the text.

Finding the family

One good way to start is to see if you can place your specimen in one of the more common families. I would not like you to imagine that finding the right family for your specimen is as easy as tripping over the cat. There are, after all, a great many different herb families in the British flora, and some of them are rather obscure. But if you can settle on the family, it will narrow your search considerably by bringing you to the right section of the book.

To help in this task, the table on page 105 sets out some of the larger and more common plant families, with a list of some of their distinguishing characters. I must stress that this is in no way a diagnostically accurate or exhaustive key. It is simply a guide to the typical appearance of the plants and their flowers in that family, using many of the features we have covered in previous chapters.

*The 8-petalled lesser celandine flowers (above) have all-round symmetry - they are **actinomorphic**, while the lipped marsh lousewort flowers (right) only have mirror symmetry - they are **zygomorphic**.*

Notes to Table: where number of petals is in brackets, it is because they are in a bell or other joined-up shape. In the DESIGN column, ARS stands for 'all-round symmetry'; 'mirror' indicates that the bottom half of the flower differs from the top half. The technical term for 'all-round symmetry' - including symmetrical bells, composites etc. - is **actinomorphic**. Flowers with mirror symmetry, including lipped shapes, are called **zygomorphic**.

And remember: this table is not complete in itself - it is designed to be used in conjunction with a fieldguide. Have your fieldguide ready to hand as you study the descriptions, so that the appearance of typical family members starts to establish itself in your mind.

TYPICAL MEMBERS OF COMMON FAMILIES

FAMILY	COLOUR	DESIGN	PETALS	FLOWERHEAD	LEAVES
Dicots					
Buttercups & crowfoots	yellow white	ARS	5	single/several	lobed/cut
Pinks & stitchworts	pink, white	ARS	5	single	opposite, simple
St John's worts	yellow	ARS	5	several	opposite, simple
Violets & pansies	mauve	mirror	5	single	simple
Crucifers (Cabbage family)	yellow, white	ARS	4	spike-shape/ clustered	various
Heaths (heathers)	pink, mauve	bell	(5)	spike-shape	simple
Primroses	yellow	ARS	5	single/several	basal
Roses, incl cinquefoils	pink, white yellow	ARS	5	several	compound
Peas & clovers	various	mirror	(5)	rounded/various	compound
Willowherbs	pink	ARS	4	spike/single	opposite, simple
Cranesbills	pink, purple	ARS	5	several	lobed/cut
Umbellifers e.g. cow parsley	white	mirror	5 tiny	umbel	compound
Borages e.g. forget-me-nots	blue	ARS	5	spike	simple
Deadnettles e.g. mints	pink, purple	lipped	(5)	whorls/spike	opposite
Figworts e.g. speedwells	blue/various	mirror	4	spike/single	opposite
Bedstraws	white	ARS	4	various	whorled
Composites (Daisy family)	yellow, white purple	composite	many	several	various
Monocots					
Lilies & irises	various	bell	(6)	various	blade
Orchids	pink, mauve whitish	lipped	6	spike	blade/oval
Water plants (miscellaneous)	white	ARS	3	various	blade

If your specimen doesn't seem to match up exactly with anything in the table, there are three possibilities.

• It may not belong to any of these families - so at least you know where not to look in the book.

• It may not be typical of the family - but if it ticks several boxes, it is worth looking at that family in any case.

• Perhaps you have misinterpreted one or more of the characters - check again.

If, on the other hand, you have successfully located the right family, it will be much easier to find your plant in the book.

Plan B

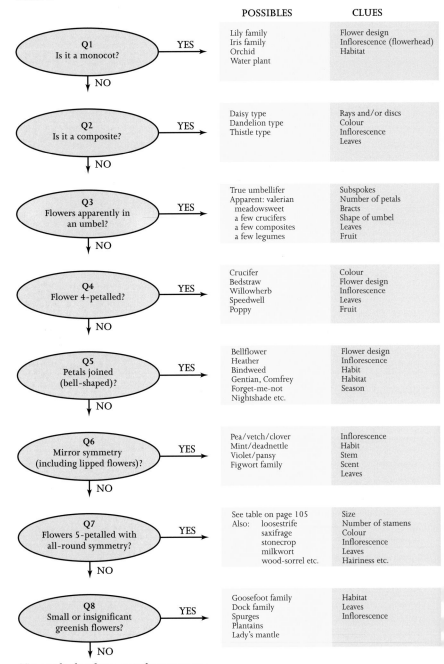

	POSSIBLES	CLUES
Q1 Is it a monocot? **YES**	Lily family Iris family Orchid Water plant	Flower design Inflorescence (flowerhead) Habitat
Q2 Is it a composite? **YES**	Daisy type Dandelion type Thistle type	Rays and/or discs Colour Inflorescence Leaves
Q3 Flowers apparently in an umbel? **YES**	True umbellifer Apparent: valerian meadowsweet a few crucifers a few composites a few legumes	Subspokes Number of petals Bracts Shape of umbel Leaves Fruit
Q4 Flower 4-petalled? **YES**	Crucifer Bedstraw Willowherb Speedwell Poppy	Colour Flower design Inflorescence Leaves Fruit
Q5 Petals joined (bell-shaped)? **YES**	Bellflower Heather Bindweed Gentian, Comfrey Forget-me-not Nightshade etc.	Flower design Inflorescence Habit Habitat Season
Q6 Mirror symmetry (including lipped flowers)? **YES**	Pea/vetch/clover Mint/deadnettle Violet/pansy Figwort family	Inflorescence Habit Stem Scent Leaves
Q7 Flowers 5-petalled with all-round symmetry? **YES**	See table on page 105 Also: loosestrife saxifrage stonecrop milkwort wood-sorrel etc.	Size Number of stamens Colour Inflorescence Leaves Hairiness etc.
Q8 Small or insignificant greenish flowers? **YES**	Goosefoot family Dock family Spurges Plantains Lady's mantle	Habitat Leaves Inflorescence

Time to look at keys, consult experts, etc.

If the table on page 105 has not helped you to move any closer to an identification, try the alternative strategy of progressive elimination. Sherlock Holmes proposed that 'When you have eliminated the impossible, whatever remains, however improbable, must be the truth'. However, in any branch of nature study, bear in mind the proviso that if it's improbable, it's probably wrong. Do keep reminding yourself that common things are common. Rarities have been found by amateurs, but it's always wise not to jump to conclusions. That said, we've all done it. I have seen more than one eminent botanist pore over some unlikely-looking plant in minute detail, speculating as to what rarity it might be . . . only to realise rather sheepishly that it's just some common species on a bad hair day.

To use the method of elimination, try following this flowchart, using the notes to each question to help you come to a decision as to whether you are going in the right direction.

Q1: Is it a monocot?

Recall the chief characteristics of monocots listed on page 32. Look for flowers with three or six petals/sepals, and for simple blade or oval leaves with untoothed margins, parallel veins and no hairs. If your plant is a monocot, go towards the end (usually) of your fieldguide. Having found the right section, study the flower design, colour and arrangement on the stem If you reckon it is an orchid, look at the distribution maps if any - some are very rare and extremely local. In the case of a water plant, note whether it is rooted in the soil below water level ('growing with its feet wet') or not, or if the plant is free-floating.

*These **common spotted orchids** show typical characteristics of a **monocot**: 3 petals and 3 sepals (but all the same colour) and simple oval leaves with parallel veins.*

If your plant is not a monocot, carry on to the next question.

Q2: Is it a composite?

A composite, remember (page 28), is made up of numerous tiny flowers arranged concentrically, like a daisy, thistle or dandelion. These tiny flowers, called florets, may consist either of flat strap-shaped petals round the edge (rays) or of little tubes in the centre (discs) or both. If both, the rays and discs may be the same colour or two different colours. For example, a daisy has white rays and yellow discs, whereas in ragworts both rays and discs are yellow.

A **composite** may have discs (central florets) and rays (outer florets) the same colour - **ragwort**, left - or different colours - **daisy**, above.

Colour is quite a good way of separating out the various sections here. Another tactic is to characterise your plant as 'daisy-like', thistle-like' or dandelion-like'. However, the yellow composites with rays only - the dandelion look-alikes - present a very real problem for learner field botanists. The best advice may be to get to grips with a few which are common in your local area and also fairly easy to identify. For example, nipplewort with many small pale-yellow flowers, corn sowthistle with its large showy blooms (see page 4) and the familiar dandelion itself are all pretty common and easy to pick out. But don't beat your brow over the hawkweeds - except for one or two, they really do demand an expert.

But if it's not a composite?

Q3: Are the flowers in an umbel?

A true umbel is a head of small flowers arranged rather like the fabric of an umbrella (see page 34). A few flowers look like umbels at first sight, but check for subspokes: if there are none, it's no good looking in the Umbellifer family. Most umbelliferous flowers are white but a few are yellow. The leaves are often much-divided, feathery or ferny (hogweed and ground elder are exceptions). What about the shape of the umbel? Is it flat-topped, mushroom-shaped, globular or what? However, umbellifers are admitted by everyone to be quite a tricky group, so don't be too upset if you can't determine exactly which species it is.

Clearly an **umbellifer,** but study the umbel shape, the leaf design and the **bracts** (small leaf-like structures at the base of a flower stalk) to make a closer identification.

If your specimen is definitely not an umbellifer at all, try the next question.

Q4: Are the flowers 4-petalled?

The largest group where 4-petalled flowers are obligatory is the Brassica or Cabbage family. These are often referred to as the Crucifers, as they typically have their four petals arranged in the shape of a cross.

Crucifers usually have a branching flowerhead with numerous small flowers, often white, yellow or pinky-mauve. The yellow ones especially are notorious for being hard to tell apart. The best clue is often the fruit. For example, shepherd's purse, an abundant weed of arable fields, paths etc., has heart-shaped pods; bittercresses have long narrow pods; honesty has translucent pods shaped like miniature badminton racquets. So see if you can find a plant with fruits already formed, lower down the stem.

Four petals in the shape of a cross *make the Crucifer (Brassica) family the first choice for this specimen. These might be cuckoo flowers, except that the leaves suggest* **large bittercress** *instead.*

Other groups with four petals as standard are bedstraws, willowherbs, speedwells and poppies. Bedstraws have small, usually white, flowers and their leaves are always arranged in whorls at intervals up the stem. The best known bedstraw is cleavers (aka goosegrass, sticky willie and other local names) beloved of children for its adhesive habit, especially on other people's backs. With willowherbs, one clue is in the stigma (the bit right in the centre of the flower, see page 22); this can be either club-shaped or cross-shaped. Speedwells are almost all blue, but fall into two main groupings: single flowers and flowers in spikes; add to this the different leaf design for each species and you should be able to pin down your speedwell.

Five petals or more? Try the next.

Q5: Are the flowers bell-shaped?

'Bell-shaped' is rather a vague term, but is used here to cover a number of families with 5-petalled flowers joined - at least at the base - to create an enclosed or partly-enclosed symmetrical space like a bell, cup or tube. So besides the bellflowers proper, we have the heathers, bindweeds, gentians, comfreys, nightshades, forget-me-nots and a few other less common ones.

Comfrey *is only one of many different* **'bell-shaped'** *designs.*

Gentian flowers are typically arranged rather like a candelabra, their true-blue, purple or sugar-pink flowers pointing skywards. Comfreys are hairy, rather coarse-looking plants which may come in a confusing variety of colours even within the same population. Forget-me-nots don't at first glance seem to belong to the bell-shaped category, but look carefully and you will see that the petals are joined at the base to make a tube, before opening out into a flatter head with the petals separated.

Not bell-shaped either?

Q6: Do the flowers show mirror symmetry (including lipped flowers)?

These are the flowers that have left-right symmetry, but not up/down. Some look symmetrical at first glance, but closer inspection reveals that the lowest petal is a slightly different shape or colour from the rest. Others give the appearance of having a 'mouth' or are described as 'lipped': these include the mints and peas (orchids too, but they should have been eliminated at Q1).

*Lipped flowers like this **bush vetch**, a member of the Pea family, have **mirror symmetry**.*

Pea flowers have a very distinctive closed shape, like a pursed or pouting mouth. The Pea family (aka Legumes) includes clovers, vetches and trefoils such as birdsfoot trefoil - the familiar eggs-and-bacon. Mints and other members of the Deadnettle family have open-mouthed flowers, which are often collected into successive whorls up the leafy stem; the stems are square and hairy, and the leaves are opposite and hairy. Figworts and violets are examples of 'mirror-symmetry' flowers which are not lipped.

Q7: 5-petalled?

If you have eliminated all the previous categories, it is likely that your plant has five petals in an all-round symmetrical flower. This is a very common pattern, including many of our most familiar flowers, and there are many variations on the theme. One way of getting closer to the correct family is to note whether

*The 5 petals of **ragged robin** may live up to its name, nevertheless it is essentially an **all-round symmetrical** or **actinomorphic** flower.*

your plant has numerous stamens - too many to count; buttercups, poppies and roses, for example, are like this, and will be found nearer the front of your fieldguide. The contrasting group has a countable number of stamens - often five or ten.

Q8: Small or insignificant greenish flowers?

Sometimes you may have trouble locating the flowers at all, because they are very tiny (making it difficult to count petals) or because, being greenish coloured, it is hard to distinguish them from other parts of the plant. On first inspection, some flowers may look confusingly like leaves or fruit. Examples are the docks, spurges, plantains and members of the Goosefoot family; lady's mantles, although actually belonging to the Rose family, come into this category too. Many plants like these tend to be found on rough or disturbed ground, so habitat can be a useful clue. Also look carefully at the leaves and fruits.

When presented with this photograph I admit I was foxed at first sight. However, although the flowers are so tiny and green as to be almost invisible, the habitat - a pebble beach - was a big clue, and the shiny leaves and sprawling habit clinched the ID as **sea beet.**

No luck so far?

If you have not done so as yet, now may be a good time to look at any keys provided by your fieldguide. Let us suppose you have found the plant you suspect is called rosebay willowherb (aka fireweed). The name, plus the fact that it has four petals and is pink suggests (by way of our Table on page 105) that 'willowherbs' is a sensible place to look. Here is a simple example of a **dichotomous** key to the Willowherb family, taken from Francis Rose's *The Wild Flower Key*. A dichotomous key is a branching key in which each couplet offers two mutually exclusive alternatives - page 101 showed a very simple example.

1   Petals present 2
    Petals absent, 4 stamens, creeping aquatic plant . . . Hampshire purslane
                                                      (*Ludwigia* genus)

2   Petals 2 - cut to look like 4,
    2 stamens, fr a bristly nut . . . . Enchanter's nightshade
                                                      (*Circaea* genus)

    Petals 4, stamens 8 3

3   Shrub, fr a berry . . . . *Fuchsia*
    Herb, fr a capsule 4

4   Fls yellow, large, seeds not plumed . . . . Evening primroses
                                                      (*Oenothera* genus)

    Fls pink (poss white), seeds with plumes of hair . . 5

5   Lvs spirally arranged, petals not equal . . . . Rosebay (*Chamerion*)
    Lvs opp, at least below, petals all equal . . . . Willowherbs
                                                      (*Epilobium*)

[fls - flowers, lvs - leaves, fr - fruit, opp - opposite, poss - possibly]

Couplet 1 asks if the plant has petals? Yes, yours has, so go to 2. Has it two petals or four? It has four, so go to 3. It is a herb, not a shrub, so go to 4; pink flowers - go to 5. The leaves are spiralling and the petals are unequal - Bob's your uncle: you know to look under *Chamerion* rather than under the true willowherb genus *Epilobium*.

When using keys:

- always read any guidelines at the beginning

- practise first with samples you know, then go on to unknown species

- don't be tempted to guess: check each feature mentioned against the plant, and

- if you don't know the meaning of a term, consult the glossary.

A herb with four unequal petals and spiralling leaves - **rosebay***: it's a no-brainer when you consult a good key like Francis Rose's.*

How many petals *- 5 or 10? Five is a much more common number for petals than ten and , if you look carefully, you will see that these* ***greater stitchwort*** *flowers have five petals, each of which is divided to the base.*

However, if you are plodding along on your own, you will inevitably arrive occasionally at a situation where you just feel like turning the pages until you come to something that looks right.

Consulting the experts

At this point, your next tactic could be to consult someone more experienced. (But beware of some whose self-confidence exceeds their genuine knowledge!) Your best bet is the website www.botanicalkeys.co.uk. This uses all the characters we have been studying, though it is a shade more technical - but by now you should be losing any lingering fear of botanical long words. If you are able to answer all or most of the questions posed, you will almost certainly emerge with the correct identification of your plant, unless it is a pretty obscure alien.

If you are still stuck, see if you can locate an expert botanist from your local natural history society, wildlife trust or countryside ranger service or the vice-county recorder for the area. Where it is unacceptable to pick the plant concerned, make good sketches and/or take good photographs (see pages 142 to 145) and supply detailed notes on every aspect of the plant to send to your chosen expert. The website of the Botanical Society of the British Isles (BSBI) invites you to send in a digital photograph by email of any plant you wish to identify.

From family to species

If you are going it alone, but have managed to locate the right family for your plant, you now need to narrow down the field still further to arrive at the correct species. As a rule, the least difficult step is moving from family (if it really is the right one) to genus; looking through the relevant pages is not such a daunting task now, and a picture page of plants that all seem to have a lot in common with your specimen may well leap out at you. Family resemblance in plants may be hard to spot, but genus-resemblance can be a lot easier. Look in your fieldguide at a page of cranesbills, crowfoots or campions, for example, and you will see what I mean. If there is a key to take you from family to genus, like the one shown on page 112, seize the opportunity and use it diligently.

But then we need to go from genus to species. This is where the fine detail comes in. What distinguishes one species from another in the field may be something very tiny. The hairiness of a leaf, the precise size of a flower, the shape of the sepals, the direction of prickles on the stem or the favoured habitat: these are all examples of the critical points that you need to observe carefully if you're going to distinguish one species from another closely related one.

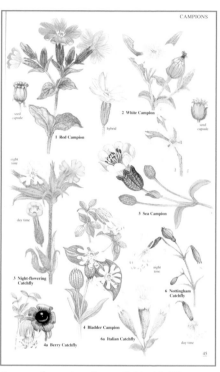

A page of campions from a fieldguide (Blamey, Fitter & Fitter) - check out the similarities in members of the same genus.

With any luck, either by diligent application of the principles, or by sensibly seeking expert help when you can't get any further by yourself, you have finally arrived at the long sought name of your plant. Now go on to the next one . . . But seriously, there is nothing like practice to build up the stock of plants you can identify with confidence. And when you find you have over time identified several species from the same family, or even from the same genus, you will recognise the next member of it much more easily.

However, ID pure and simple is not the only important thing. Working through the questions will have obliged you to look carefully at all the features we have discussed - flower design, leaves, hairiness and all the rest. You have carried out genuinely botanical procedures and in the process you have, I suspect, learned a lot more about plants and enjoyed doing it. Definitely more fun than playing 'snap'.

GETTING INVOLVED

While there is a lot of satisfaction in being able to identify an individual plant, there is even more fun to be had in making a habit of it. Later on we will be looking at some organisations you can join which are specifically for field botanists. However, you may already be taking part in activities which involve plants; this chapter will encourage you to make the most of these, as well as suggesting a few you may not have considered. Some of these can be enjoyed on your own, while others are about getting together with people who share your interest. Besides field trips where finding and identifying plants is the chief purpose, you can make wild flowers the focus of other activities such as painting, photography, crafts and conservation work.

FIELD TRIPS

Once you have developed some reliable methods for distinguishing the plants you find, and have mastered the identification of a few common species, it is time to go on a field trip.

Keeping good company

We can divide field trips roughly into three kinds. The 'top' level is an excursion organised by experienced field botanists for the express purpose of finding, identifying and recording the plant species in a given area, for example those run by the organisations we look at in the next chapter, such as the BSBI. Quite a few of such meetings are flagged as 'beginners welcome', so take them at their word and go along (don't forget to contact the leader of the meeting in advance for booking and other details). Some of the business at a meeting like this will inevitably go over your head at first; however, many botanists remember what it was like to be a novice themselves and most will be only too happy to answer your questions and pass on the benefits of their experience. Botanists are pretty friendly people and some have a vast all-round knowledge of the natural world and/or an intimate knowledge of the local area. Do take advantage of such expertise if you can - and don't be afraid to take notes: even if they don't make total sense at the time, they may later prove useful and interesting.

More pairs of eyes mean more plants will be spotted.

Next are various kinds of general nature walk. Some of these are run by organisations such as Natural England, the National Trust or Countryside Rangers in areas such as National and Country Parks. Others are more informally arranged by local natural history societies, Wildlife Trusts and so on. These may be held in nearby SSSIs (Sites of Special Scientific Interest), nature reserves or well-known local sites. On any of these nature walks you may expect to be guided by someone with plenty of botanical knowledge, though their personal speciality might be birds, insects, whatever. So by going on one of these excursions, you will learn a lot about the countryside in general and quite a bit about plants in particular.

Apart from expeditions held at particular times, many local authorities, tourist organisations and even public and private companies lay out way-marked nature trails for visitors to follow. These will usually have a map and an information board at the starting point. It is then up to you to take the walk at your own pace, enjoying the scenery and examining the plants and other wildlife at your leisure.

When you see a board like this, you know at once that this area will be worth exploring, and that help is provided for you to make the most of it.

The third kind of field trip - but last by no means implies least - is the one you organise yourself, to be undertaken either alone or in the company of a few like-minded friends or family members. We shall look at an imaginary excursion of this kind, to demonstrate not just how to go about it, but also how much you can learn and progress in your botanical studies by careful observation and detailed recording of your findings.

Planning your own field trip

- I suggest setting aside just an hour or so for your first field excursion. You don't want so brief a session that you hurry through without studying your plants carefully, but nor should you become so burdened with data that discouragement threatens to set in.

- Choose a small area you consider 'wild'. It could even be a long-neglected corner of your garden or of a local park, playing field or churchyard. Better, if you can manage it, would be a rural hedgerow, field headland or meadow, streamside or woodland edge.

This small area, where a stream and footpath run under a railway bridge, with fields on one side and rough ground on the other, proved to contain a great variety of plants.

- Take with you a good fieldguide, a notebook and your hand lens if you have one. Wear sensible footwear. That's it for equipment: botanising's not a gear-intensive pursuit. However, it is a good idea to wear old clothes; you might hesitate about getting down on your hands and knees - or even lying flat out - to scrutinise the details of a small plant when wearing your brand new designer trousers.

- Fence off the chosen area - but just in your mind's eye. As it might be: 'From the tree, inside the wall and round as far as the road'. At this point, you might also refresh your memory, if necessary, about the Country Code (if you are not familiar with it, see page 137).

- Have a look round and try to make a rough assessment of the habitat. Is it cultivated land, waste ground or semi-natural? (Very few habitats in Britain today are entirely untouched by the hand of man - or woman.) Is the situation sunny or shady or a bit of both? Is the ground dry or damp? Have you an idea as to whether the soil is acidic or basic? Does the site have any special character such as a water feature or any sign of pollution factors?

- Open your notebook and write in today's date, and where you are exactly (nearest feature named on a map should do, a grid reference is even better if you want to get professional). Add your observations about habitat.

- Now work your way systematically around the site, listing the plants you can identify with some certainty, writing notes on the ones you need to work on. Include any grasses, ferns, trees, etc. that you can distinguish from each other, even if you're not going to attempt identifying them just yet.

- It's not a bad idea to note down also any other aspects of nature that catch your eye. The natural world is in reality a seamless garment - an ecosystem, if you like - where all the parts are related in various ways. And the fun of botanising isn't confined to making a list of upfront flowers. Perhaps you keep seeing the same insects on the same species of flower: does that insect play a vital part in the plant's lifecycle, you may wonder. While quietly studying a plant, you may notice birdsong that was previously drowned out by chatter or traffic noise. All kinds of wildlife may impinge on your consciousness if you keep your eyes and ears open.

Insects visiting the flowers you are studying - this is a six-spot burnet moth on thyme, one of its food plants - will add to the interest of the trip.

SIDE ORDER

I was out botanising one day at a spot not far from houses and roads, looking at the plants growing beside a shallow stream that drained into a a small lake nearby. My eye was suddenly caught by a flurry of movement just a few yards away: three young stoats had come hustling and tumbling down the stream, so engrossed in their play that they didn't even notice I was there. I stood stock still pretending to be just a feature of the wild furniture, and watched entranced as they carried on with their antics oblivious. They raced and chased and rolled each other upside down in the steam - dry land and shallow water were one continuous habitat to them - and behaved for all the world like a trio of puppies. I wouldn't have missed it for anything. But if I'd set out to look for 'young stoats having a ball in a stream', I have a feeling I might have looked forever without finding them.

A family of **stoats** *at play. If you see a stoat or weasel flashing past, keep still and wait: if it has spotted you it may well pop its head out from the undergrowth to take another look at you.*

After a while, your notebook might look something like this.

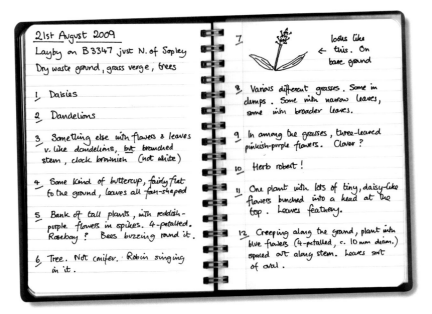

Notebook entry:

21st August 2009
Layby on B3347 just N. of Sopley
Dry waste ground, grass verge, trees

1 Daisies

2 Dandelions

3 Something else with flowers & leaves
   v. like dandelions, but branched
   stem, clock brownish (not white)

4 Some kind of buttercup, fairly flat
   to the ground, leaves all fan-shaped

5 Bank of tall plants, with reddish-
   purple flowers in spikes. 4-petalled.
   Rosebay? Bees buzzing round it.

6 Tree. Not conifer. Robin singing
   in it.

7 [drawing] looks like ← this. On bare ground

8 Various different grasses. Some in
   clumps. Some with narrow leaves,
   some with broader leaves.

9 In among the grasses, three-leaved
   pinkish-purple flowers. Clover?

10 Herb robert!

11 One plant with lots of tiny, daisy-like
   flowers bunched into a head at the
   top. Leaves feathery.

12 Creeping along the ground, plant with
   blue flowers (4-petalled, c. 10 mm diam.)
   spaced out along stem. Leaves sort
   of oval.

Let's look more closely at your findings and see what else you could do to firm up your list.

1. Daisies. I'm sure you're right, but what makes you sure you're right? What's the 'jizz' that immediately shouts 'daisy!'?

2. Dandelions. Here it's even more important to be sure, because - unlike daisies - dandelions have a host of imitators, as you've clearly realised.

3. Well spotted - it would have been easy to shrug off these plants as 'just more dandelions'. You've hit on the key points, that dandelions don't branch, and they have white 'clocks'. If, as I suspect, the plants here have tiny scales up the stems (where another plant might have leaves) it would be cat's ear, which is a very common yellow composite, often growing in the sort of place where dandelions might be found (though starting to flower later in the year). Look up cat's ear in your fieldguide to see if this fits.

*You never know, you might be lucky enough to find a **butterfly orchid** in your patch. **Cat's ears**, also in this picture, are much more likely, however.*

4. This sounds like creeping buttercup - check with your fieldguide.

5. Rosebay seems very likely (and rosebay is pollinated by bees) but check with the book - are you sure it's not foxglove? Or purple loosestrife? If you worked through the key on page 112, though, this should be an easy one.

Creeping buttercups, docks and plantains - *three likely finds in many plots.*

6. If your fieldguide includes trees you could have a stab at it by comparing leaves, bark, flowers/fruit if any are visible. However, many trees have been planted (often in the remote past) and are not native to Britain, so you may need a specialist tree book. Robins are one of the very few birds singing in August.

7. It's well worth making a sketch, especially if you don't have a book with you and/ or the plant is hard to describe in words. You've got all the essentials in the picture, and any botanist would tell you it's almost certainly ribwort plantain. Check with the book. The leaves might suggest a monocot: how do you know it's a dicot?

8. Grasses are admittedly difficult for the beginner. You have picked out two characteristics that are definitely useful for ID, namely the width of the blades and the habit of the grass - clumped ('tufted') versus solitary or creeping. However, there is a lot more to learn, so you may well want to leave grasses to a later stage in your botanising.

*Close-up of **ribwort plantain**. The colours of the anthers - the most noticeable part of the flower here - help to distinguish the plantains: ribwort's are pale brown, greater plantain's purple, both the coastal species have yellow anthers.*

9. Red clover is very common in lots of grassy habitats, but again check with the book to be certain.

10. Of course you should know this one if you studied it carefully earlier in this book. But it might just be the rarer shining cranesbill (look closely at the leaves) or if the flowers are larger or smaller it could be another of the common cranesbills, so check with your fieldguide.

11. If you have looked carefully at the flowers to confirm they are the composite type, then this is probably yarrow, but it might be sneezewort or feverfew. These will probably be all on the same page in your fieldguide, so it shouldn't take long to find out.

Yarrow flowers (left) and **sneezewort** flowers (above) are very similar, but the latter are much bigger and less crowded.

12. It would be worthwhile to make a few more notes here: it sounds like a speedwell, especially if the lowest petal is smaller and paler than the other three, but there are several common speedwells (it's not unusual to find two or three different species growing alongside each other), so check all the details.

Two different speedwells: **thyme-leaved** (above) and **germander** (right). Quite a few plants have the epithet 'thyme-leaved' (Latin: serpyllifolia). It means the leaves are small, untoothed, opposite ovals like those of thyme. Germander speedwell has larger toothed leaves and the flowers have a distinctive white 'eye'.

So you've got four direct hits: daisy, dandelion, rosebay and herb robert. Plus four 'probables': cat's ear, creeping buttercup, ribwort plantain and red clover. The 'possibles' - yarrow and speedwell - need further investigation. You've also made a start on trees and grasses and noted the presence of birds and insects. In other words, you've had a successful botanising session!

Keen to carry on from here? Why not repeat the exercise in a contrasting habitat? Suppose your first trip was to a piece of waste ground; your next might be to a river bank or a wood. Now you can make some comparisons. What plants do you find that were not in your original plot? Are there any plants found in both habitats and if so, what does that tell you about those plants? Is the number of different species in your second habitat larger or smaller than in your first - and what does that tell you? Have you perhaps got a handle on beginning to predict what plants you might find where? Trying to answer these questions will increase your confidence in the business of botanising and, with any luck, sharpen your curiosity to the point where you want to take part in an organised field trip with expert botanists on hand to start filling in the gaps. Go for it.

Could this be a good place to botanise? Several microhabitats - stone wall, gateway, pasture, amenity trees, and in the background deciduous woods and rough grassland - suggest it probably is.

RECORDING WHAT YOU SEE

Field notebook

In the previous section we looked at how you might jot down the findings of your field trip in a notebook. This is one of the ways you can record the plants (and other things) you see, and all keen field botanists will have a notebook somewhere about their person at all times. Hoping to remember enough about the plants to record them once you get home is an exercise doomed to failure - even a list of half a dozen or so known species can be taxing to carry in your head for any length of time. Where doubtful species are concerned, detailed field notes, sketches, photographs etc., *made on the spot*, are essential if you intend to consult various botanical books at leisure in the comfort of your own home. Don't forget to jot down the date, location and habitat assessment as well.

Nature diary

There are other reasons besides identification for keeping records, and other ways of keeping them as well as (not instead of) a field notebook. Many outdoors enthusiasts, as well as having a field notebook, will maintain a nature diary, perhaps a fresh one for each year, in which they enter all the plants, birds, animals, insects etc. they have observed. This might also include such things as weather events, geological features encountered, tips from seasoned naturalists, or whatever piques your interest. As before, each entry needs a date, a location reference and habitat notes. Such an 'all records' diary serves a number of purposes. In the first place, it is a permanent

Smooth hawksbeard *is a very common species, but difficult to pin down with certainty until you are quite familiar with the yellow composites. Good photos, sketches and notes would be essential if you wanted outside help to ID it.*

record: field notebooks have a nasty habit of getting wet/grubby/torn/mislaid and the handwriting, though legible enough for short-term memory, may appear as an indecipherable scribble at a later date.

Secondly, a nature diary is a wonderful thing for reviving memories of a delightful experience or situation. If it contains notes on all kinds of wildlife - sights, sounds, scents etc. - it can transport you straight back to that scene as you sit at home on a dark wet winter's night. It is also very useful for the purposes of comparison. 'I'm sure I've seen that plant before somewhere - was it round about June last year?' You can look back to June last year and there are all the details to compare with the plant you saw today. Other kinds of comparison can be fascinating too. Two habitats, for example, that seemed similar at first sight, but turned out to have rather different communities of plants, may provide lots of food for thought. Or a single habitat recorded in different seasons or over successive years may actually turn out to be a valuable record for conservation and other purposes.

SIXTY YEARS OF RECORDS

The following letter from Jean Combes appeared in BSBI News in January 2007.

Botanists have a long tradition of recording the first plants of spring - celandines, violets, primroses or whatever. Gilbert White of Selborne was one such person as was also his friend Robert Marsham of Norfolk. Marsham kept a set of records which he started in 1736 and which were continued by seven generations of his family until 1947.

I followed this tradition as an eleven-year-old child, despite living in London at that time. When I grew up, however, I was embarrassed by these juvenile diaries and I threw them away and started all over again. I have now been recording the leafing dates of four tree species in Surrey for the past 60 years, of which the last 40 years have been records from Ashtead which lies 3 km south of Epsom. The four tree species are:
Horse-chestnut *(Aesculus hippocastanum)*
Common Lime *(Tilia x europaea)*
Oak *(Quercus robur)*
Ash *(Fraxinus excelsior)*

It never occurred to me my data would be of interest to anyone else until I read a newspaper article in 1995. This stated that Dr Tim Sparks, a government scientist, was collecting such records for possible indications of climate change and I sent him my data.

In a recent Woodland Trust article (July 2006) Dr Sparks said my oak-leafing dates had been used in two government publications and he added the following - 'Jean's data is probably unique in phenological recording and as far as we know is the longest record by a single person anywhere in the world'.

This illustrates perhaps the surprising value of keeping simple records and might encourage other BSBI members to emulate.

Reprinted by kind permission of BSBI News

Postscript: In the 2009 New Year Honours List, Jean Coombes received an OBE for 'services to phenology' (dates of seasonal phenomena).

This is not a book about trees (or the ferns, lichens and mosses that grow on them), but Jean Combes' efforts could easily have been applied to forbs instead - or yours might.

Lifelist

Virtually all keen birdwatchers maintain a 'lifelist' of every new species they spot, perhaps with the underlying hope that in time they will have seen every bird on the British list. Botanists, of course, have a great many more species on their potential list, and their chances of seeing every single one are virtually nil. Even the most senior botanists will generally admit to quite a few species they still haven't encountered. But a lifelist is a great thing to attempt, so long as one remembers there is a lot more to field botany than 'plant twitching'. Keeping such a list needs to be done in a systematic way, however; even a few hundred records simply jotted down higgledy-piggledy could be a nightmare to sort into scientific order. One suggestion would be to enter just dates and locations briefly in your favourite fieldguide or other comprehensive handbook, thus cross-

Lily of the valley *is not too uncommon in ash woods and on limestone pavements, but as often as it is native in these places it is a garden escape or even planted deliberately. Would you add it to your lifelist if you weren't certain it was native?*

referencing them to fuller details in your nature diaries. The Wildflower Society provides pre-printed lists of plants for use as records over a year's botanising.

Official recording

If you feel you want to 'give something back', you may consider submitting your records to an official body, where they can be used to help compile distribution maps, vice-county lists and other statistics. For the purposes of biological recording, the British Isles are divided into **vice-counties** which were marked out in 1852 when record-keeping was first formalised. These comprise 112 roughly equal areas, based on the British counties of the time; Irish vice-counties were added later (the natural history community, unlike the political one, makes no distinction between northern and southern Ireland). These vice-counties do not change when successive governments redefine administrative county boundaries to suit themselves. Each **vc** (vice-county) has its own botanical Recorder to whom records can be submitted. See the BSBI website for details.

The national Biological Records Centre accepts records from anywhere in the country, and many counties also run their own records centres for all types of records; looking online is probably the best way to establish contact with these places.

If you are going to make an official submission, you need to be sure it is absolutely accurate; most bodies say they would prefer no record at all to one that is in any way dubious. So if you think you have found a genuine rarity, for example, or have made some observations of wider interest, you should (a) have all the details of date, exact location (grid reference), number and condition of plants etc. ready to hand and (b) preferably enlist an expert to confirm your finding.

*The distribution of **clustered bellflower** is clustered (sorry) mainly in the vice-counties of central southern England such as Hampshire and Gloucestershire, but it may also be found much further afield if you're lucky.*

If you come upon this rarity, **small cow-wheat** *(most likely in Northern Ireland or Scotland) someone in the botanical world will be delighted to hear from you. But it's at least a hundred times more likely to turn out to be common cow-wheat, so check and double-check with your fieldguide.*

RUM RECORDS

How would someone come to submit an incorrect record? Ignorance, carelessness, jumping to conclusions, failing to double-check the relevant points - these are all possible reasons for unintentional errors. But would anyone submit false records *deliberately?* In a case described as 'the greatest scandal of twentieth century botany', someone did - and that someone was an extremely eminent and respected Professor of Botany at what is now Newcastle University. Careful investigations by later botanists have confirmed that a number of the rare plants supposedly 'discovered' by Professor Heslop-Harrison on Rum and other Hebridean islands in the 1930s and 40s - plants otherwise unknown in Scotland or even in Britain as a whole - were in fact planted there by their self-appointed discoverer. The whole fascinating story was revealed in Karl Sabbagh's 1999 book *A Rum Affair*. (The botanical grapevine had been quietly disseminating its suspicions from the start, but was reluctant to embarrass the Professor's family or indeed to wash its own dirty linen in public.)

Yet Heslop-Harrison made many major contributions to botanical studies and did genuinely discover a number of notable rarities in the Hebrides: what moved him to perpetrate such a monstrous fraud? It has been suggested that the very esteem in which he was held, and the autocratic power he exercised over his Department, 'went to his head.' He had a pet theory that the Hebrides had been spared by the last Ice Age, the time when most of the then British flora was frozen out of existence. The plants he 'discovered' would have added substantial weight to his tenaciously - some would say obsessively - held theory. Did he believe his theory to be so incontrovertible that it justified him in planting the evidence himself? Or is there some other explanation?

Why not read Sabbagh's book and see what you think?

CONSERVATION AND THE ENVIRONMENT

If you are genuinely interested in plants and wild nature in general, the last thing you will want to do is damage the very conditions in which those plants flourish. So care for the environment and for individual plants, creatures and habitats within it should be right at the forefront of your concerns when botanising. The Botanical Society of the British Isles (BSBI) has drawn up a Code of Conduct which is followed by its members, and has also been adopted by the Wild Flower Society and by Plantlife for their own members. (See page 150 for more about these organisations.)

A **bluebell** is the symbol - these days highly stylised - of the Botanical Society of the British Isles. But native bluebells may be subject to hybridisation with the escaped or planted garden species Spanish bluebell. Learning to tell them apart is a good way to start understanding hybridisation.

Code of conduct

The key points in the Code of Conduct are as follows:

- Flowering plants, ferns, mosses and liverwort, lichens, algae and fungi all require protection so that they may be enjoyed by future generations as you are enjoying them now.

- All wild plants are given a measure of protection under the laws of the United Kingdom. Under the Wildlife and Countryside Act of 1981, it is illegal to uproot any wild plant without the permission of the landowner or occupier. Under the Theft Act of 1968, it is an offence to uproot plants for commercial purposes unless authorised to do so by the landowner. So on no account dig up bluebells or primroses, even for your own garden.

- In SSSIs, National Nature Reserves etc. even the occupiers may not remove or destroy plants without specific permission.

- The Wildlife and Countryside Act contains a list of endangered species which may not even be picked, let alone uprooted, without permission. Most orchids are high on this list.

- It is also an offence to plant certain aliens which may be a threat to native wildlife, unless you have first obtained a licence. Many botanists also deplore the habit of planting daffodils, snowdrops etc. from gardens along the hedgerows and byways nearby; the reason is that non-native varieties can hybridise with native species and thus spoil the native gene pool. The same argument applies to sowing non-native seeds of wild flowers, even in your own garden. If you want to sow a 'wild flower garden' do check that the seeds are sourced only from UK populations.

It is acceptable to many people to pick plants for pleasure, for study or as food for personal use. Common law allows for traditional customs like picking blackberries and mushrooms, cutting some holly, ivy and mistletoe at Christmas or gathering sloes and dandelions for home-made wine. You may exercise these rights in places where you have a legal right to be, though pay attention to local bylaws. Even so, always be careful only to pick from large populations (with flowers, count at least twenty of them first, before picking just one) and never take more than you absolutely need. If you have any

Orchid *(in this case, early purple orchid) - Don't pick!*

suspicion at all that the plant in question may be rare - if it looks unusual, you cannot find it in a book, or distribution maps suggest it is uncommon - then play safe: do not pick it at all. (Certain additional cautions and precautions apply if you are using plants for particular purposes, such as photography, pressing, displaying, ingesting etc. These topics are covered in later sections.)

Sloes, *the fruit of the blackthorn, are used to flavour sweet gin, as opposed to dry gin which is flavoured with juniper berries. However, while blackthorn is very common, the survival of juniper is more in doubt, so it would be most unethical to take juniper berries from the wild (assuming you could find any).*

PICKING AN ARGUMENT

Should wild flowers be picked? Earlier in this book you have been encouraged to pick a flower to study. Yet we have also seen how avid collectors have brought about the scarcity or even extinction of some plants. It is now illegal in most circumstances to uproot any wild plant, and 'leave wild flowers for others to enjoy' is a very sound maxim. However, the current politically-correct position seems to be that taking anything from the wild is to be condemned out of hand. I can't help wondering if, in the long run, this might have the opposite effect from that intended, by making the natural world so 'forbidden' that people feel excluded from it? Has the pendulum swung too far?

The majority of us now live in towns and cities, and spend only a small proportion of our time out of doors. An opportunity to study the finer points of plants in detail, and to contemplate their beauty at leisure, may only arise if plants are sometimes picked and brought indoors. After all, too, one cannot walk in open countryside without often (if sadly) treading on flowers. Could we end up being forbidden ever to leave the path lest a wild plant should be crushed underfoot? Rather than impose a blanket ban, the emphasis could be on teaching people to behave responsibly - no uprooting, picking only from large populations of common flowers, taking no more than needed, and so on. Note that this only applies in places like hedgerows and open countryside, however; flowers should not be picked at all in nature reserves and other protected areas - if these were ever to become seen as 'pick-your-own' facilities, the results could be disastrous.

The true enemy of wild plants today is not picking but pervasive human activity: climate change, pollution, intensive agriculture, demands on land for housing and industry, monocultural conifer plantations and the indiscriminate planting of verges and seeding of odd bits of land with garden flowers and dubiously-sourced seed. Instead of vilifying the town-

*A busy roundabout planted with **wildflower seedmix**. This particular seed was reliably sourced - I checked with the Council - but many seed merchants use seed from abroad; this introduces strains or even species which may contaminate the local gene pool.*

dweller - and especially the child - who wants to bring the natural world into their home with a jar of buttercups and daisies, we could take a more pro-active attitude. Support the maintenance of wild areas and oppose schemes that threaten them (join a conservation movement), look hard at the impact of our own lifestyles, and learn more about plants so that we are aware what needs to be done.

Access

The so-called right to roam does not entitle you to go anywhere, anytime. (The situation in Scotland differs slightly from that in England and Wales.) In principle, you can go anywhere in open, uncultivated countryside which is not restricted by farmers' schedules, military movements, health and safety regulations, landowners' licensed requirements and a good few other things. Your dog must be kept under close control and you must not cause any damage, break any laws (including local bylaws) or invade any gardens, fields of crops or specially protected sites. In short, make sure before you start that you are allowed to go where you are going and to do whatever you are proposing to do.

A beautiful day to go botanising!

ON THE MAP
If you intend going off the beaten track, you need a map (a compass and/ or GPS are handy too). A large scale Ordnance Survey map - 1:50,000 (the former 'one inch' maps) or better still 1:25,000 - is not only a great help in taking your bearings in an unfamiliar landscape, it's a good aid to botanising as well. Besides roads, hills and rivers, it will show you footpaths and rights of way, National Trust and Forestry Commission boundaries, coniferous and deciduous woodland, cliffs and quarries, marshes, lakes and ponds, parks and farms, mudflats, tide limits and much more. To a botanist, it's talking habitats! Before leaving home, you can use the map to discover what habitats are represented in the area and plan your route taking in all those you want to explore. Incidentally, if you want to study the potential of an area before spending money on a complete map, you can - for personal use only - print off a map of your chosen area at *www.ordnancesurvey.co.uk*

Sensible behaviour

For your own safety and well-being, there are a number of other aspects of being out of doors that should engage your attention.

The weather. If you are going to be away from your base or vehicle for more than minutes, you should either wear or carry clothes for the worst the weather is likely to throw at you. This is especially vital if you plan to be well away from dwellings or go up hills, or if the weather looks at all changeable. It goes without saying that sturdy footwear is essential; a waterproof jacket, an extra sweater or fleece, and a dry pair of socks will also prove to be godsends if the weather deteriorates. Don't forget the opposite sort of weather either: botanists are well-known for sporting sunhats (which make pretty good rainhats too) and they know what they are doing. Suncream and fly repellent will also be much appreciated on a hot summer's day. Add a water bottle, a snack, a first aid kit and your trusty fieldguide . . . and you need a comfortably-fitting rucksack to carry it all in.

If you are planning serious hill-walking, of course, you will need considerably more preparation than this, so consult a specialist guidance manual.

Safety. However enthusiastic you may be in your search for wild plants, always be mindful of your personal safety. Keep away from the edges of cliffs, quarry faces, unstable banks of rivers and deep mud or bogs that might steal your wellies and leave you to walk home in your socks - those dry ones you put in

*It may look fairly solid, but the foreground of this picture is a **bog** that means business. With practice, you will learn to recognise the vegetation that suggests firm ground which you could use as stepping stones to cross a boggy area.*

the rucksack. (The trick with mud is to keep on the move.) If you carry a pair of binoculars, you can use them to examine plants that are out of reach on a high ledge or the other side of fast-flowing water. If you are botanising near a road, always keep an eye and ear open for traffic. And remember that signs saying 'Beware of the bull', 'High voltage cable' and the like are not erected for their entertainment value.

Ticks are almost inevitable in some areas of countryside at some times of year. Keeping as much of your body covered as possible - trousers tucked into socks, long sleeved tops etc. - is the first line of defence. However, examine your whole body when you get home, just in case. What appears to be a little pink pimple or - at a later stage - a blackish lump, might be a tick, even if you don't feel any itching or pain. Assuming you're not squeamish about these things - come now, you're a naturalist - look at said lump through your x10 lens. If you see eight wiggling little legs (ticks are related to spiders), then you've picked up a tick.

The recommended method for dealing with ticks is with a special 'tick tool'. This is intended to remove the tick without causing the stress that might make it regurgitate blood into your flesh, thus increasing the possibility of transferring infection. (Though I have to say that attempting to use the tool single-handed on a fleshy, hard-to-reach site can seriously stress both of you.) If you don't have a tick tool handy, try the following procedure.

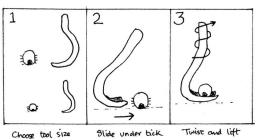

Choose tool size   Slide under tick   Twist and lift

Using a tick tool.

Slap a good dollop of vaseline onto the offending creature, making sure it's completely covered, and leave for ten minutes or so (under a plaster, if you like). Wipe off the vaseline, seize the tick with tweezers as close to your skin surface as possible, and pull. Believe me, this works a treat; trying to detach the tick before thoroughly suffocating it is liable to leave the head still under your skin, festering away to cause great irritation and possible infection. (If you're a Buddhist, consult your spiritual adviser.)

Very occasionally, a tick may transmit Lyme disease. Should you develop a rash and/or flu-like symptoms after a country walk, see your GP. Lyme disease is treatable with antibiotics if caught early - if not, it can end up being a very serious condition.

Lightning. If you are caught in the open during a thunderstorm, do not shelter under a tree! Avoid tall structures, loose rocks and anything metal. If you have to sit it out, sit on your rucksack or a pile of dry clothing and curl yourself up to make as small a target as possible, until the storm abates.

Mobile phones. Although a wonderful invention and certainly to be carried on field trips wherever possible, mobiles are not infallible. Even if it is in full working order, you may still find yourself in a spot where the signal is poor to non-existent. In keeping with Sod's Law, this will turn out to be the very place where you are desperate for assistance. The golden rule is not to get yourself into any situation which could only be resolved by means of a mobile.

*A patch of old **woodland** anywhere might contain all these species: pink purslane (often in white, as here), bluebells, speedwells and pignut, among others.*

BOTANISING AT HOME

Lest you should feel intimidated by the dangers and difficulties of botanising far from home, you might take heart at the large variety of plants recorded by one botanist on his own housing estate in East Suffolk. This estate of about sixty houses dated from the 1960s and contained lawns with different mowing regimes plus verges maintained by the council. In all, he counted 59 different species, including nine wild grasses and sedges, twelve composites, five speedwells, three violets, two forget-me-nots, a daffodil and a single plant of meadow saxifrage. The last is a very nice find even in the wild, let alone in a town garden. How many species might there be in your patch?

The Countryside Code

Besides the Code of Conduct for botanists, all visitors to the countryside should observe the Countryside Code. For full details see *www.countrysideaccess.gov.uk*, or for Scotland, *www.outdooraccess-scotland.com*. Some (paraphrased) points especially relevant to botanists are:

• Let someone know where you are going and what time you will be back.

• Unless you are sticking to a way-marked trail - and probably even then - take a map and know how to use it. On a way-marked trail, be sure to follow the signs.

• Leave gates as you find them - open or closed. Farmers have various important reasons for both positions. Remember the countryside is a working environment.

• Don't walk through growing crops. Go round the edge, or use any paths provided. Use gates and stiles to cross boundaries, where available.

• Botanists cannot be commanded always to stick to paths, or they wouldn't get much in-depth botanising done, but when you stray off the beaten track, take extra care not to cause any damage (or get lost).

• Don't interfere with machinery or livestock. If an animal seems to be in trouble, tell the farmer. Remember that cows with calves at foot, for example, herds of bullocks or groups of horses and ponies can be quite dangerous if approached too close.

• Take your litter home, including any unwanted food - don't even think of feeding it to those sweet-looking horses over the fence. If they kick and injure each other in their excitement to get at the food, whose fault will that be?

• Don't light casual fires, drop matches or in any other way risk starting a fire. Be especially careful in dry weather.

*The ruins of **old buildings** can be seen in this picture, and no signs of intensive grazing, so there might be interesting plants, including relics of cultivation, to be botanised.*

• When driving in the countryside, go slowly and carefully on narrow country roads. Give way to livestock on the move, pedestrians, horseriders etc. Don't block gateways or entrances or obstruct other traffic when you park. If you are walking along a country road, remember to keep to the right, facing the oncoming traffic, and take extra care on blind corners.

Should you find on your excursions some plants interesting enough to warrant reporting, be careful how you go about disseminating the information. A well-known botanist wrote up his findings for his local Naturalists Club as follows:

I recently found a place on a roadside where someone had evidently emptied the rubbish from the bottom of a parrot cage. Here were growing sunflowers, opium poppies, canary grass and a couple of fine big cannabis plants, all of which are included in bird seed mixtures.

Weed - *a plant whose virtues have not yet been discovered?*

A few days later he was startled by a headline in his local newspaper which read:
OPIUM AND CANNABIS FOUND ON A LEICESTERSHIRE ROADSIDE.

THE PLEASURES OF PLANTS

It may be that your purpose in learning to identify wild flowers is to build on an interest you already have. At the same time, you could find that studying plants leads you on to fresh ways of enjoying them. The more aspects of wild plants you get involved in, the more you will learn about them, and the more you learn, the deeper your involvement will become. Here is a selection of ideas for encouraging and widening your knowledge and enjoyment.

Fresh flowers

A small vase of wild flowers on your table is a wonderful reminder of an outdoor trip, a stimulus to other people who see your display and also an opportunity to study them at leisure. I am well aware that the picking of wild flowers is a controversial matter: see page 132 for a discussion on this question. But I believe that so long as you remember the rules about only picking a few common flowers which are plentiful in the spot where you find them, you might gather a bunch now and then to grace your home without feeling guilty. Besides the codes already mentioned, some points to bear in mind are:

This vase of flowers and grasses was composed solely of common and locally abundant native plants and garden escapes.

- Rather than pick all of one kind, choose a selection of different flowers, perhaps with a colour scheme or botanical classification in mind. This avoids the possibility of decimating a population of a single species, and also allows for a more interesting arrangement.

- Garden flowers intended for cutting are specially bred to live long after being severed from the parent plant, but some wild flowers barely last until you get them home. It is obviously a waste of time and a waste of flowers to pick ones like this. The best known example is probably poppies; as Robert Burns had it,

> 'But pleasures are like poppies spread
>
> You seize the flow'r, its bloom is shed.'

Cranesbills (*Geranium* species) and speedwells (*Veronica* species) are also disappointing groups for picking and you will no doubt find some others out for yourself by trial and error. On the other hand, some last and last, while others seem (perhaps to a biased eye) to look just as good even when they have 'gone over'.

- For goodness sake don't pick any invasive species, however attractive those Himalayan balsam flowers may look! As your rejects and dead flowers are likely to be thrown out into the garden, compost or landfill site, you are only helping to fuel their plans for world domination.

- You will need a suitable container for bringing home flowers that you intend to display, so that they don't get spoilt on the way. A zip-top polythene bag into which you can blow air to keep blooms from being crushed is one solution. A large plastic box is another, though more bulky to carry. So long as the container is properly sealed, it is better not to add water - it will only slosh about on the journey and probably do more harm than good. If transporting plants upright, a cushion of damp moss at the bottom can be useful.

Don't pick! Not because it's rare, but because Himalayan balsam is highly invasive by means of its spring-loaded seeds.

- If your plan is to collect seeds for planting in your garden, remember that the very same rules apply as to picking flowers. It is a similar situation with wild berries: don't strip branches bare but pick here and there, leaving the majority for the local wildlife to consume

Drying and pressing

Grasses and sedges, rather than forbs, are often the best candidates for drying per se. These will simply dry themselves if put in a waterless jug and once dry will last virtually for ever. The seedheads of some plants can also look most attractive in a dried flower arrangement. Some flowers from the wild do dry well, however, if secured upside down, hanging free from a beam or shelf in a warm room. The pretty mountain everlasting (*Antennaria dioica*) is as good as its name suggests, but it is unlikely to be found in abundance, so you will have to be content with just one or two. Drying can also be done by other methods such as silica gel and microwave drying.

As far as pressing is concerned, there are three main methods. The first is the good old-fashioned method of putting the flowers between sheets of newsprint or blotting paper, or between the pages of a redundant telephone directory, placing a stack of heavy books on top. The paper will need to be renewed every so often as it soaks up the moisture. The second way is to buy or make a flower press. It is not easy to find good-sized flower presses on the market - most are small ones designed for children. However, making your own really is child's play. You need:

Mountain everlasting *in unusual profusion. You might pick just one of these for your collection, so long as they are not in a conservation area - and it won't even need pressing.*

- two pieces of good quality plywood, A4 or whatever is your desired size

- several sheets of corrugated cardboard (cut from a box, say) the same size

- twice that number of sheets of blotting paper (double-thickness kitchen roll - not too quilted - will do the same job)

- four or six strong plastic clamps that you can buy in any DIY store

- a labelling system (it's depressingly easy to forget the details of something you pressed weeks ago)

The diagram opposite shows how to assemble your press.

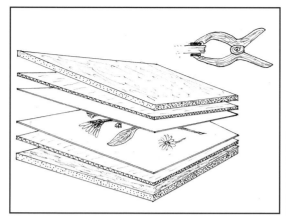

This diagram shows only one layer, but you can have several, up to the capacity of the clamps. A small square press can manage with four clamps, one at each corner; a larger rectangular one is better with six.

The third, high-tech, method of pressing is to buy a microwave press and follow the instructions. A short spell in the microwave will miraculously convert your flowers from fresh to dried in a matter of minutes, and this method has the additional advantage of preserving the colour better than do traditional methods. However, be warned: it is very easy to scorch the flowers if left in too long, even to damage the equipment itself. So err on the shorter side of time in the microwave - you can always put them in again if they aren't quite 'done'.

Lay out your specimens for pressing in such a way that they look natural (not bent at odd angles, for example). Arrange petals carefully so as to show the flowers at their best, perhaps including a head-on and a side-on view. Do the same with the leaves, maybe showing both upper and undersides. If you need to prune away some leaves or flowers to avoid a cluttered or untidy result, take care to do it in a way that still preserves the natural appearance of the plant.

LADY'S BEDSTRAW

Dried flowers have a much longer history than simply for aesthetic or botanical purposes. Before the days of carpets (and nasty aerosol room sprays) it was customary to strew the floors with plants that dried quickly and also gave off a pleasant scent This could be done afresh every day - and if harder work than hoovering, at least it must have been a more pleasant task. One plant whose common name reflects a similar historical use is lady's bedstraw (*Galium verum*). There is an old legend that this plant was used for bedding material at the nativity of Jesus and that it received its golden colour on that occasion having previously - like all the other *Galium* species - been white-flowered. Certainly it was used in some parts of the world as the herb of choice for lying-in bedding, owing to its hay-like scent and its reputation as a styptic and flea-repellent.

As to the uses of dried and pressed flowers, you may take the artistic route and combine them into wild flower pictures, or you may want to start your own herbarium and assemble a collection of interesting specimens in a file or folder. If you have a really puzzling specimen that you would like to consult an expert about, properly dried material is often preferred to sending fresh material through the post.

Lady's bedstraw is yellow, but all the other bedstraws are white.

Photography

If you are already into photography, you will probably need no further spur to include wild flowers among your subjects. In any case, it is a good idea to gain some proficiency at wildflower photography so that you can keep a record of what you have seen and also for occasions when you need to show someone else for the purposes of identification. There is not space in the present book to go into detail about how to take such photographs, so if this is your intention you would be best advised to get a specialist book on the subject.

A super photograph starring a single wood anemone flower.

Some general points to remember about plant photography in the wild are:

- Especially if ID is your purpose, take several shots from different distances and angles, to ensure that all aspects of the plant, such as stem, leaves, inflorescence, individual flowers etc., are all shown clearly.

- Get as close as your camera will allow for some shots, but make sure you can still focus properly. It can be very annoying to get home and find that your close-up is just a blur of colour and little else.

- Consider putting a piece of dark or light card behind your specimen so that it shows up well against the background. On the other hand, you may be anxious to show your plant in its natural setting and want to alter it as little as possible.

- But do not 'garden'. That is to say, do not push other plants roughly out of the way - or worse still, remove them altogether - in order to make your chosen plant stand out. You may inadvertently be destroying plants that are rare or delicate and that will not recover from your thoughtless treatment of them. On the other hand, you may end up making a rare plant stand out all too well, advertising its presence in a way that will ultimately harm it.

- As well as not gardening, be careful not to trample down other nearby plants by accident. Keep all disturbance to a minimum and endeavour to leave the spot exactly as you found it.

With a digital camera, you can compile a 'virtual herbarium', by transferring the images to your computer, labelling them with name (when you succeed in identifying them), location and date, and arranging them in scientific order. Another possibility, if you have a scanner, is to scan in the live plant (be careful not to damage the platen glass - sandwich the plant between clear sheets) and proceed as above. Hours of both learning and pleasure are guaranteed for the long winter evenings.

Drawing and painting

Much of what has been said above applies also to preparing to draw or paint a plant in situ: most importantly, take care always not to harm the plant itself or any other plants (or indeed insects, birds, whatever) in the vicinity.

Also, as above, if serious drawing and painting of plants is on your agenda, you would benefit from having a book devoted to the subject. A word of warning here though, especially if you're buying sight unseen, such as online: there are two distinct types of books on drawing/painting plants. One type is concerned with **botanical illustration**, which is a highly technical skill, demanding a very thorough knowledge of plants and extremely precise ways of portraying them so as to elucidate their characteristics and act as an aid to identification. Botanical illustration can be a career path, and you may come across advertisements for full or part-time courses in the subject.

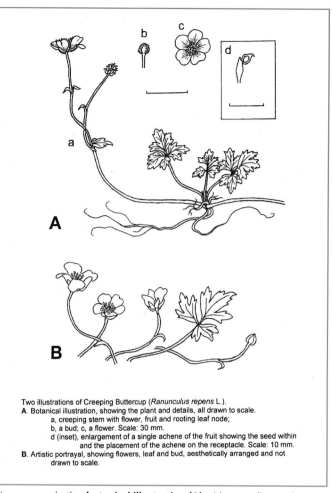

Two illustrations of Creeping Buttercup (*Ranunculus repens* L.).
A. Botanical illustration, showing the plant and details, all drawn to scale.
  a, creeping stem with flower, fruit and rooting leaf node;
  b, a bud; c, a flower. Scale: 30 mm.
  d (inset), enlargement of a single achene of the fruit showing the seed within
      and the placement of the achene on the receptacle. Scale: 10 mm.
B. Artistic portrayal, showing flowers, leaf and bud, aesthetically arranged and not
  drawn to scale.

*Here you see both a **botanical illustration (A)** with every diagnostic
detail clearly shown, and an **aesthetic drawing (B)** which gives a general
'artist's impression' of the plant, creeping buttercup.*

This absorbing and challenging occupation could be exactly the line you are
keen to pursue. However, if what you want is to draw and paint flowers for
aesthetic reasons alone - to amuse yourself, delight your friends and so forth,
then you need a different kind of book, one that is aimed at the amateur (in
the best sense of the word) and that will almost certainly take you through
the basic principles of drawing and painting - materials, techniques and
so on - before concentrating on the application of those principles to the
representation of plants, with suggestions on how to make attractive pictures
featuring natural subjects.

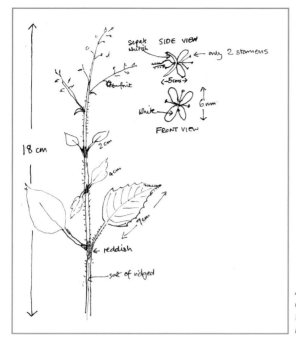

*A **quick sketch**, done on the spot, picking out the important points for identification.*

Even if you don't see yourself as a budding artist, it is a good idea to practise making sketches of plants in the field: an accurate picture can be worth at least a hundred words of description where ID is concerned. Here is an example of the kind of quick sketch you might make on the spot of an unfamiliar plant.

You'll see that dimensions and colour notes need to be added, and that a two- or three-part drawing can give more information. Draw the whole plant from ground level up, showing growth form, branching, shape of inflorescence, leaf position etc. Add a drawing of an individual flower and possibly of a leaf too. Don't neglect features such as hairs - these may be crucial to ID and it would be frustrating to find you hadn't noted their presence or absence. Can't draw? You'd be surprised what you can do with a bit of practice: naturalistic art is as much about looking as it is about technical skills. (What plant is this? Clue: It is described quite fully earlier in this book. Answer at the end of the chapter.)

Crafts and consumables

A number of crafts besides painting and pressing can make excellent use of wild flowers. **Dyeing** with native plant materials is one countryside skill that is currently enjoying something of a revival. **Nature printing** may appeal to those who doubt their artistic prowess. You probably remember making potato prints at primary school: many other plants can be used to make naturalistic prints once you have mastered the techniques.

Bilberries (aka blaeberries, whortleberries, wimberries etc.) are an under-appreciated natural resource. They make super pies, preserves and even liqueurs, and are reported to have significant medicinal properties, as with most purple fruits.

The edibility (or otherwise!) and palatability of plants is a topic well beyond the scope of the present book. However, since the first publication of Richard Mabey's *Food for Free* in 1972, there has been a substantial growth of interest in the products of the countryside which, not so very long ago, was the common knowledge of all country-dwelling people.

Home-made **cosmetics and natural remedies** are other avenues for exploration if this is where your interest lies. However, do bear in mind that 'natural' is not a synonym for 'harmless': meticulous identification is essential before using any wild plants in this way.

Wildflower gardening is becoming increasingly popular. Not only is a wildflower garden beautiful in its own right, it is a wonderful way of attracting other wildlife, especially butterflies, into your garden. Charles Flower's book (yes, that's really his name) *Where have all the Flowers Gone?* should put you on the right track.

The **'green revolution'** may involve us in using plants in highly imaginative ways for fuel, fertilisers, textiles, furnishings and a hundred other purposes, as they were used before the industrial era began. Who can predict how important these uses might become in the world of the future?

NATURAL BENEFITS

A study undertaken in 2008 (Berman, Jonides & Kaplan) demonstrated the benefits of spending time in natural surroundings. Two groups were first given the task of recalling lists of random numbers in reverse order. One group was then sent out to spend time in an arboretum, while the others took a walk down a busy city street. Both groups then returned to re-take the random numbers test. The group who had been wandering through the trees showed a 20 per cent improvement on the task, whereas the street-walkers showed

The epitome of green tranquillity.

no significant improvement. The researchers found that even just looking at images of natural scenes as opposed to urban ones produced an improvement on the test. They concluded that - as other studies have also shown - nature gives our involuntary attention a rest from the stimuli that bombard it in busy, stressful situations and restores us to a calmer, less stressed frame of mind. The colour green is in itself believed to be innately restful and refreshing.

Admittedly this is a meadow created from commercial seedmix (the cornflowers give it away) but still a delightful sight.

Conservation work

With a related eye to the future, all over the country - in towns and cities as well as rural areas - there are conservation projects crying out for volunteers. Tree planting, scrub clearance, path repair, plant recording and monitoring: you name it. Where there is work to be done in the field of conservation, volunteers will always be welcomed with open arms. From Plantlife, the national body for plant conservation, down to your local nature reserve or neighbourhood pressure group, you will find numerous opportunities to take part.

It's a two-way street. While you are doing your bit for plants and the country-side, you will be meeting congenial like-minded people. Conservation projects can often involve the whole family, or utilise the teamwork of youth groups, college clubs, local residents associations and so on. At the same time, you benefit from the healthy exercise, enjoy the open air and the scenery, and increase your knowledge of plants and other wildlife, together with your understanding of how they all interact.

Answer to sketch query: enchanter's nightshade (*Circaea lutetiana*) - see description on page 112.

Enchanter's nightshade*: not easy to describe in words, perhaps, but a good sketch or photo clarifies all the important points.*

SOURCES OF HELP

You are not alone! Field botany may not have the high profile currently enjoyed by birdwatching, for example, but it has enthusiasts all over the country - indeed all over the world - if you know where to look.
In this final chapter, we consider organisations you might like to join to further your interest in and knowledge of wild plants. We also look at a selection of helpful books and websites. In conclusion, we see how field botany is a pursuit which anyone can enjoy - and may even make a major contribution to.

ORGANISATIONS

To feed your enthusiasm for wild plants, and to meet people on the same wavelength, you could consider joining a local or national wildlife group, perhaps a local branch of the Wildlife Trusts or a local natural history society. Many of these have a botanical section; for example, there is a botanical arm of the London Natural History Society.

There are several organisations at a national level which welcome new amateur members but they have slightly different emphases. The **Botanical Society of the British Isles (BSBI)** *www.bsbi.org.uk* is the chief authority on matters of field botany, recording and conservation. The BSBI holds field meetings throughout the country, quite a few specifically aimed at newcomers. The **Wild Flower Society** *www.thewildflowersociety.com* is very friendly and helpful to beginners. **Plantlife** *www.plantlife.org.uk* is an organisation dedicated to the conservation of wild plants in their natural habitats; it has many schemes encouraging people to get out in the field.

Each part of the British Isles has its own government body with overall responsibility for conservation and related matters. These are: **Natural England, Scottish Natural Heritage, Countryside Council for Wales, Northern Ireland Environment Agency** and in the Republic of Ireland, the **National Parks and Wildlife Service.** Some of these produce helpful books, booklets and guides, and the information on their websites may be of use to you.

The **Royal Botanic Gardens** at Kew and Edinburgh, among others, have collections of British natives where you can view the plants growing in conditions that replicate their original habitats, and they have an educational role with regard to plants, often offering talks, guided walks or courses in botany.

*A view of the Scottish Heath Garden at the **Royal Botanic Garden Edinburgh**, where native plants grow in a realistic setting.*

The **Natural History Museum** in London, besides having a herbarium of more than six million specimens, runs projects involving the public. Your local museum may also have a botanical section. Any of these organisations will be glad to help you with botanical queries, or will be able to point you in the direction of the best person to approach.

The **Field Studies Council** is an environmental educational charity with seventeen centres around the country. Identification is a key part of their courses on plants, many of which are suitable for beginners and some for family groups. They also publish many relevant books and pamphlets.

Course members at at a Field Studies Council centre learn to identify the plants they have found.

BOOKS, MAGAZINES, WEBSITES

Books

As we have already seen (page 96), the majority of books on wild flowers per se are fieldguides of one kind or another, consisting mainly of plant illustrations with accompanying descriptive notes. We have also mentioned local floras and checklists, which are very useful when you are concentrating on a particular geographical area. Most of these books will have a bibliography which leads you to other books on related topics.

The BSBI publishes handbooks on groups of plants that are especially hard to distinguish **(critical groups)**, including volumes on Roses, Crucifers, Umbellifers and Dandelions. These are not, needless to say, books for beginners, but when you get to a stage where you feel you need more detailed information than your fieldguide can provide, you may want to purchase one of these books, or perhaps the **Plant Crib** which deals with many distinctions that even experts have difficulty with. The **New Atlas of the British Flora** (2002) gives distribution maps for every species as at the year 2000. There is even The **Vegetative Key to the British Flora** (2009) for identification of plants which are not in flower. The Field Studies Council produces some helpful charts for beginners, and **A New Key to Wild Flowers** in the Aidgap series for the more dedicated student.

*Experienced botanists study a **hybrid rose** to decide which species have contributed to it.*

For books on botany-related arts and crafts, edible plants, plant language, lore and history you probably can't do better than a Google or Amazon search. These will, of course, usefully throw up books which are out of print as well as more recent publications.

Magazines

There are no magazines on general sale exclusively about wild plants, but all the societies mentioned above

*Many people would vote **grass-of-Parnassus** one of the most beautiful of all our native flowers. Find it in damp, rather alkaline grassland, mainly in the northern half of these islands.*

publish their own regular newsletters or bulletins which are highly informative and often well illustrated. Several other publications carry botanical articles ranging from popular to specialist, including British Wildlife, BBC Wildlife and BBC Countryfile. Your local paper may run a column of Nature Notes, giving you hints on what to look out for in your immediate area.

Websites

The only totally reliable website for identifying plants is www.botanicalkeys.co.uk, which is run by the BSBI. This demands a certain amount of knowhow to use it constructively, but once you have absorbed the contents of the present book, it should serve you very well. The BSBI website, www.bsbi.org.uk, has pictures, descriptions and up-to-date distribution maps, all very helpful. It also includes a rather jolly Knowledge Test (click on Field Skills) where you can test your ID skills on photographs of plants labelled 'easy', 'average' or 'hard'.

A relatively new website which promises well for the future is www.iSpot.org.uk, which is run by the Natural History Museum in conjunction with the Open University. It covers all aspects of the natural world and, among other things, you can post a photograph of a plant for other members to identify (some of the members are very experienced botanists).

www.thewildflowersociety.com also has quizzes, competitions, lists of plants and so on. At www.plantlife.org.uk you will find details of nature reserves, conservation campaigns and a host of FAQs. In my experience, one should

FLOWERY FORENAMES

It is well known that some girls' names have a cycle of fashions - according to Katherine Whitehorn, they come round again when the last great-aunts who bore them have passed away. Flowery names such Ivy, Violet, Myrtle and Lavender are in abeyance at the moment, but Daisy, Poppy, Lily and Jasmine are now back in the top fifty favourite forenames. Heather, Hazel, Veronica and Rosemary are stalwarts that have never really gone away. Other popular names may not be recognised as having a flowery root: Margaret is from *marguerite*, French for daisy; Betony is the common name of a woundwort; Bryony, Cicely and Sorrel are all plant names. Why does no-one name their baby girl Crocus, Cowslip or Samphire? Or perhaps they do. Boys (in this country, at least) do not seem to be called after flowers at all: an interesting sociological phenomenon. (Although plants can be called after boys: ragged robin, herb robert and jack-by-the-hedge spring to mind.) Basil might seem to be the exception, but in fact both the name of the herb and the name of the boy derive independently from the Greek word for king. What are the chances for Woodruff, Darnel or Galingale - they all seem to have a suitably masculine ring?

approach with care other websites that purport to identify wild plants by means of photographs etc. The photographs themselves are often super, but the botanical knowledge is sometimes a little hazy.

Another useful site for botanists is www.summerfieldbooks.com which has a vast variety of botanical and other natural history books, and also sells a variety of hand lenses. The site www.field-studies-council.org is the one to consult for courses in botany, and www.wildlifetrusts.org is the place if you want to join your local branch.

BOTANISING FOR ALL

Can anyone botanise? Since botanising only means looking at plants growing wild 'in the field', the answer of course is yes. You don't have to be a time-served botanist to botanise. What's more, botanising can be combined with virtually any other outdoor activity - walking, climbing, birdwatching, conservation work, to mention just a few - except perhaps sailing and flying . . .

There are professional botanists who work in learned institutions, studying the finer points of plant biology, working with plants for medical use, developing commercial strains of crops and a hundred and one other topics. Academic botanists may or may not be interested in botanising in the field out of office hours. There are also dedicated amateur field botanists who may spend most of their free time recording all the plants in a particular area or charting the fate of rare species over the years. But there are many other people who start by knowing nothing of botany, before their interest is awakened by the weeds in their garden, or the flowers they see on a country walk.

Birdwatching as a hobby has had a lot of exposure in recent years, with books, press articles and television programmes all helping to inform and entertain those interested in birds. However, people curious about wild plants have not up till now been so well-served. Why is that, I wonder? Viewed as a hobby, botanising has some advantages over birdwatching - the most obvious being that plants *keep still* while you get a good look at them (though see page 46). As we have seen, so long as you observe the code of conduct, you may even take home the occasional plant so as to study it at greater length, or to paint or press it, thus preserving it for posterity. It would be very unwise nowadays to try that trick with a bird, even assuming you could catch one.

As there are at least four times as many kinds of plants in Britain as there are birds, there's never a dull moment. At any time, you may light upon one you've never seen before, perhaps in the most unlikely of spots - and the detective work of identifying it starts off the fun all over again. Besides the natives, there is the fascination of casuals (here this year, probably gone the next), plus garden relics and escapes which may persist for many years after their garden ancestors have been replaced by this year's fashionable flowers.

Eyebright *species are, to put it mildly, a difficult group to ID. At the last count there were 23 separate species, many of which hybridise with each other, but to the uninitiated they all look pretty much alike.*

Once you begin to get the hang of identifying individual species, you might widen your field of interest to take in subspecies and hybrids too. Sedges and rushes are not really very difficult to get to grips with (and every bit as beautiful as 'flowers'), and once you have done so the grasses are not quite so daunting. Then there are the non-flowering plants: the ferns, mosses and so on . . .

There are very few physical restrictions on botanising. While it may be great fun to go up mountains and see alpine plants, for example, mountaineering is not for everyone and there are many interesting plants to be seen at sea level. It helps to be physically fit (and a day of botanising here and there will help

The beauty of **cottongrasses** *- some prefer to call them cottonsedges, which is what they truly are - is splendidly displayed in this photo.*

to make one so) but it is not essential. There are many older botanists whose walking stick comes in very useful for hooking down branches or dragging in waterplants that are too far from the shore to reach without waders. With an all-terrain wheelchair, it is possible to botanise even when not on your own two feet.

A BLIND BOTANIST

John Gough of Kendal was a brilliant nineteenth century botanist who was totally blind. Wordsworth wrote a poem in tribute to him, and Coleridge had this to say: '[he is] not only an excellent mathematician but an infallible botanist and zoologist . . . as to plants and flowers, the rapidity of his touch appears fully equal to that of sight, and the accuracy greater.' It is said that Gough frequently used his tongue to examine the finer points of plants and surpassed all of his colleagues in what he was able to discover by his unorthodox methods.

Try shutting your eyes and examining a rose without the benefit of sight. How many other senses can you employ to tell you about its nature?

Botanising requires very little in the way of special equipment or clothing - a fieldguide, a lens and a sturdy pair of boots will get you started. And wild plants are everywhere, once you begin to look: in the cracks of city paving stones and old walls, in parks and gardens, by roadsides and under hedges, as well as in the 'real' countryside. What's more, some exciting botanical discoveries have been made by ordinary amateur botanists.

A new British species

In 2003, Cornwall County Council civil engineer Matt Stribley was inspecting a bridge over the River Camel near Wadebridge. Mr Stribley had always been interested in botany, but only started seriously studying plants four years ago. 'I had finished inspecting the bridge when I went to have a look at a rocky area,' he explained. 'I stuck my head inside this crevice and saw a plant I didn't recognise.' He took a sample to local botanical recorder Rosaline Murphy, who sent the specimen to the Natural History Museum. The plant was originally thought to be brittle bladder-fern (*Cystopteris fragilis*), a widespread UK species. But the museum identified it as diaphanous bladder-fern (*Cystopteris diaphana*) - a species common in southern Europe, but not known in the UK.

'The brittle bladder-fern is quite rare in Devon and Cornwall, so I thought that was quite exciting,' Mr Stribley said. 'When it turned out to be something new to Britain I couldn't quite believe it.' Museum scientists think it has been there for thousands of years and was previously mistaken for brittle bladder-fern. 'Britain is arguably the best biologically known piece of land in the world, so the discovery of a new native species is an increasingly rare and very exciting event,' said Fred Rumsey, the Natural History Museum botanist who identified the fern. 'It is amazing to think that this plant could have been here waiting to be discovered since just after the last Ice Age. It just goes to show how important amateur naturalists are in helping us to discover more about British biodiversity.'

Diaphanous bladder-fern, a British native fern first discovered in 2003, is believed by experts to have been here unrecognised for thousands of years.

A single gateway seems to have a welcoming aspect where botany is concerned. How much more promise is offered by three gateways!

INDEX

Note: page numbers in *italics* refer to illustrations

knotweed, Japanese   6, 11, 12

labellum   29
lady's mantle   111
Latin/scientific names   90-2, 94–5, 98
leaves   38–9, 40
    alternate   39, 40
    arrangement   39, 100
    autumn colour   27
    basal rosette   39, 42, 52
    description   103
    dicot   32
    life cycle of plant   49
    lotus effect   38
    monocot   31, 32, 107
    opposite   39, 40
    protective modification   42
    relation to stem   39
    shape   39
    veins   32
legumes see peas
lens   20, 41, 90, 118, 135, 154, 157
leopard's bane   65
life cycle of plant   49–50
life story of plants   49–55
lifelist   127–8
light spectrum   27
lightning   135
lily   32
    identification   105
    Kerry   88
lily of the valley   127
limestone   62, 63, 66, 67, 73
ling   53–4, 55
lipped flowers   29, 104, 116
loosestrife   23
    purple   35
lotus effect   38
lousewort   86
    lipped marsh   104
Lyme disease   135

Mabey, Richard   146
magazines   152–3
maps   133
marsh marigold   24, 67, 86
Marsham, Robert   126
meadowsweet   43, 67, 86
microhabitats   124
microwave press   141
middens   87
milkwort
    colour variation   26
    sea   79
mint   26
    identification   105, 110
    scent   43
mirror symmetry   28, 29, 104, 110
mistletoe   131
mobile phones   136
moisture, soil   61, 62
monkeyflower   25, 29

monocots   29, 31, 32, 90, 91
    families   105
    identification   105, 107
mosses   17
    sphagnum   67
motorway verges   83
mountain everlasting   140
mountain plants   44, 63
movement by plants   46–7
mushrooms   131

names of plants   6
naming of plants   89–114
    see also classification of plants; fieldguides;
        keys
National Nature Reserves   131
National Parks   117
National Parks and Wildlife Service (Republic
        of Ireland)   150
National Trust   117
National Vegetation Classification scheme   65
native plants   11
Natural England   117, 150
Natural History Museum (London)   151, 153,
        157
natural history societies   117
natural remedies   146
natural surroundings, benefits   147
nature diary   125, 126
nature reserves, protection of plants   132
nature trails   117
nature walks   117
nectar   23, 42
needs of plants   60–4
Neptune plant   18
nettle   14, 21
    hairs   42
    leaves   39
    soil conditions   87
New Atlas of the British Flora   152
New Flora of the British Isles (Stace)   97
A New Key to Wild Flowers   152
new species   157–8
newspapers 92, 138, 152
nightshade   109
    deadly   42
    enchanter's   65, 148
nipplewort   53, 108
non-flowering plants   17, 90, 91
Northern Ireland Environment Agency   150
notebook   118, 119, 121, 124–5

Open University   153
OPR (Optical Plant Recognition) software   98
orchids   6, 32
    bee   30, 83
    birds-nest   27
    butterfly   30
    common spotted   107
    design   30
    early purple   131
    fen   69

ACKNOWLEDGEMENTS

I should like to thank the following people. For their early encouragement: George Ballantyne and Joanna Thomas. For reading various drafts and making helpful comments and suggestions: Alistair Godfrey, John Grimshaw, Liz Lavery, Ron Youngman, Sue Atkinson, Siobhan McGuinness. For the initial cover design: Elisabeth Jardine. For technical advice: The Writers' Workshop. For offering me a range of brilliant photographs from which to select the illustrations so integral to this book, and giving me lots of help and advice besides: Polly Pullar. For providing various additional images, often waiving a fee on the grounds that it was a worthwhile project: all the people and organisations mentioned in the picture credits. For combining text and illustrations into such an attractive design: Frank Lee of Lodge Graphics. And for turning a raw manuscript into a published book with professional skill, energy and unfailing good humour: Shirley Greenall at Whittet Books.

CREDITS

The author and publishers would like to thank the following individuals and organisations for their kind permission to use their photographs and other materials for the illustrations in this book.

Images are referenced by page number first with the position of the image on the page shown in brackets (T-top, B-bottom, L-left, R-right, TL-top left, etc.)

Images

The images were supplied by Polly Pullar with the exception of the following:

Photograph of author by Angela Fendley; 5(R), 6(BL), 8(B), 30(T), 44(B), 47, 53, 55(R), 64, 82, 90, 96, 116, 117, 118, 124, 132, 137, 138(B), 139, 152(T) Faith Anstey

12(BL) Lorne Gill/SNH; 18(B) unknown; 54 Peter Birch; 56 Graham Day, www.habitas.org.uk/flora; 57 SNH; 61 (maps) Philip's; 72(L) Philip's; 73(R) Natural England; 75, 79(T), 80(T) (dotmaps) by kind permission of BSBI; 80(B), 83(L) Peter Birch; 88(L) Zoë Devlin; 88(R) Wilton Lewis; 94 Peter Birch; 97(T), 100, 114 Domino Books Ltd; 115 Liz Lavery; 120 Andrew Cates; 133 Gordon MacPherson; 138(T) Nabokov (free licence); 141 Robert MacPherson; 144 Barbara Sumner; 148 Michael Valentine; 150(T) (logos) Botanical Society of the British Isles, The Wild Flower Society, Plantlife; 150(B) Lynsey Wilson/RBGE; 151 Sue Townsend/FSC; 157 Andrew Leonard; 158/159 Derek Harper

Text

77 List of 'commonest plants': by kind permission of The Countryside Survey, Lancaster Environment Centre

112 Extract from *The Wild Flower Key* by Francis Rose © Francis Rose, 1981, 2006. Reproduced by kind permission of Frederick Warne & Co.

126 *Sixty Years of Records*; by kind permission of BSBI News

The plants pictured outside the main text are:

Page 1 (title page)	Northern marsh orchid and daisy
Page 3 (contents page)	Common twayblade
Page 4	Corn sowthistle
Page 169	Common centaury
Page 173	Hogweed